GOD
AND
POWER

"Keller's book draws attention to our 'apocalyptic unconscious,' which lately has irrupted in various ways onto the political scene. . . . Keller's point that theology can no longer afford to ignore these powerful manifestations of the apocalyptic serves as a wake-up call. . . . Keller proposes resistance through imaginative counterapocalyptic strategies that value different sorts of power and courage. All who share her searching question, 'Can something divine still come to us?' will find challenge and stimulation in this book."

—**JOERG RIEGER**, Professor of Systematic Theology,
Perkins School of Theology, Southern Methodist University

"In a time when declarations of moral absolutism, ruthless imperialism, and apocalyptic vindication abound, Keller's pursuit of loving and meaningful multiplicity in the face of uncertainty provides a valuable rejoinder. These reflections engage the brutal legacy of apocalyptic belief without flinching and yet offer ways to read the ever-ambiguous Book of Revelation richly, creatively, anew, and as vital to what she has called a theology of becoming."

—**LEE QUINBY**, Harter Chair in Humanities,
Hobart and William Smith Colleges

GOD
AND
POWER

COUNTER-APOCALYPTIC JOURNEYS

CATHERINE KELLER

FORTRESS PRESS
MINNEAPOLIS

GOD AND POWER
Counter-Apocalyptic Journeys
Copyright © 2005 Augsburg Fortress. All rights reserved. Except for brief
quotations in critical articles or reviews, no part of this book may be reproduced
in any manner without prior written permission from the publisher. Write:
Permissions, Augsburg Fortress, Box 1209, Minneapolis, MN 55440-1209.

Unless otherwise noted, Scripture quotations are from the New Revised Standard
Version Bible, copyright © 1989 by the Division of Christian Education of
the National Council of the Churches of Christ in the USA, and are used by
permission.

Cover art: © 2004 Corbis
Cover design: Brad Norr Design
Author photo: Shelly Kusnetz
Interior design: Zan Ceeley

Library of Congress Cataloging-in-Publication Data

Keller, Catherine,
  God and power : counter-apocalyptic journeys / Catherine Keller.
    p. cm.
  Includes bibliographical references and index.
  ISBN 0-8006-3727-5 (pbk. : alk. paper)
  1. Christianity—United States. 2. Christianity and politics—United States.
I. Title.
  BR526.K445 2005
  277.3'083—dc22

                                          2004030789

The paper used in this publication meets the minimum requirements of
American National Standard for Information Sciences—Permanence of Paper for
Printed Library Materials, ANSI Z329.48-1984.

Manufactured in the U.S.A.
  09   08   07   06   05   1   2   3   4   5   6   7   8   9   10

Contents

Preface
Theopoetic Justice

One of the stock figures of American kitsch has been the bearded street prophet wearing his end-of-the-world sandwich board. As the end of the twentieth century approached, a *New Yorker* cartoon version featured this theme: "The Apocalypse is coming. Or do I have it confused with the millennium?" Even dating the millennium was confusing: January 1, 2000—or 2001? Both went by not with bangs but with whimpers. Then there exploded, in eerie proximity to the millennial transition, the emergency numerologically encrypted as "9/11."

The world did not end, nor has a better world dawned. But if there are no signs of imminent rapture, a dangerous spirit of apocalypse did infuse the national response. The spirit has a double nature, religious and political. And it is looking a lot like a gigantic genie that cannot be put back into the bottle, even when the national leadership changes.

There is nothing wrong with a strong interaction between faith and politics. The biblical text is saturated with what we call "politics"—with national liberation remembered and expected, with law for daily life, with material care for the poor. In the United States the interaction of church and state—within the formal terms of "separation"—has at its best enabled an unprecedented multiplication of religious and secular viewpoints. That pluralism keeps this culture boiling at the edge of chaos. And it is not only definitive of our democracy, but apparently healthy for religion, which by every statistic thrives in the United States. The practice of pluralism at once constrains the cruel exclusivisms that perpetually tempt Christianity and stimulates a vigorous mix of spiritual creativities. This interactive tension between religion and state is perhaps more honestly described as a *productive difference* than as a separation.

The danger arises when the difference between worship and citizenship dissolves into an idolatrous blur. The *power of worship* morphs into the *worship of power*. It is this metamorphosis that we have seen manifest with new aggression in the theater of world history. It has set the stage for the century. Perhaps there is a perverse advantage in such overtness. It brings latent tendencies and hidden agendas into consciousness, and therefore, where possible, into public debate and democratic self-awareness. This book contributes an added irritant to the consciousness-raising process. It tries to make culturally recognizable what we may call our *apocalyptic unconscious*. Its figures of beast and whore, of warrior messiah and virgin bride, dance at the edges of our collective rationality, stirred up by any feeling of catastrophe. They circulate in a dream of the end of the world or of its new beginning. It is a dream living just below the surface of our national self-image.

I have long been tracking the politics of apocalypse. When in the 1980s I took in the symbiosis of President Reagan, with his finger on the nuclear button, and the religious right, with its Hal Lindsey–hailed end of the world by imminent thermonuclear exchange, I was chilled: not by any biblical predictions of doom but by the new power to *make them come true*. The literal belief in the Armageddon scenario could no longer be confined to a cultural margin. Was it functioning as a self-fulfilling prophecy? I felt that oldstream Christians had better stop ignoring John's Apocalypse. Where I had gone to seminary, we had never studied that text. But it wasn't going away!

Multiform in its mutations, explosively mingling the political with the religious, productive of the most revolutionary and the most reactionary movements of western history, the apocalypse unveils an absolute enmity, an Evil that will collapse in the final confrontation with (our) messianic Good—which is always Coming Soon. I didn't grow up with that sort of Christianity. It cost me considerable effort to understand its passion without merely demonizing it in reverse (as in "those who accuse others of Evil are the True Evil!"). Gradually I came to recognize its pattern pervading even the politics that shaped

me, such as the women's movement of the 1970s and 80s. I began to
encourage my students, many of whom seek ordination, to pull the
apocalypse out of the shadows and into dialogue.

Believe me: I would have been content to leave that work back in the
last millennium. However, as the meditations of this book suggest, we
as a people have hardly begun to come to terms with our apocalyptic
unconscious. And as therapists tell us, what we do not work out, we *act
out*. I am not claiming that the "born-again" quarter of the population
who expect the imminent end are unconscious of the apocalypse; on
the contrary, they live it out knowingly. But such beliefs would remain
relatively harmless if it were not for their perilous fusion with the
political drive of the nation. The idolatry and the threat to democracy
arise in the fusion of messianism with power. It is a doubling characterized by a spirit not of dialogue but of duplicity.

On the one hand, a tendency in the United States toward political
messianism burst into a new, undisguised manifestation, symptoma-
tized by presidential promises to "rid the world of the evil-doers," to
"call evil by its name," and to expect of course the undivided loyalty
of Christian evangelicals. On the other, a secular strategy of global
dominance was formulated by the Project for a New American Century, the neocon think tank. They found in the crisis a great opportunity: we were to use our military hegemony to stabilize a chaotic world
for our geopolitical and economic interests. But this *Pax Americana*
is offered with idealistic zeal. Thus apocalyptic God-talk fused with
unapologetic empire.

What's wrong with this picture? For starters, this combination is
evangelically absurd. The biblical Messiah comes to *beat* the empire,
not to *join* it! The empire in the Book of Revelation *is* the evil: the
"great city," the whore of Babylon, is an allegory for Rome and its
politico-economic domination of the known world. And yet the sort of
Christianity being invoked for two decades in increasingly high places
bases itself upon a fundamentalist reading of the Bible.

Not surprisingly, the self-contradicting fantasia of this amalgam
that we may call "messianic imperialism" has neither reduced evil nor
enhanced stability. But I think this contradiction goes deeper. It can
reveal something of ourselves—our intertwined, neither merely good
nor merely evil, neither purely private nor purely public, selves. Rather
than waiting for the Bush Jr. administration to implode, let us avail
ourselves of the opportunity: the irruption of the apocalyptic uncon-

scious into visibility provides an opening, albeit a tragic one, for a more responsible political alternative to emerge.

So I am suggesting that we heirs of the hope for liberation and a just, bountiful new age, a "new creation," meditate upon these contradictions—whether we consider ourselves "secular," "spiritual," or "religious." These contradictions are our own. And they are legion. Messianic imperialism always wears an aura of invincible strength but in fact marches oxymoronically toward collapse. It magnifies the specifically American contradiction that results when church and state begin to merge. This contradictory situation reflects the tension between the two faces of postmodern empire: the first being the globalization of the economy, the other the project of global dominance. The globalization of the economy is inherently transnational and comfortable with a pagan cosmopolitanism. The project of global dominance is inherently unilateralist, inspired by a nationalist warrior-messianism. These two faces blur in a white haze of entitlement—but unsustainably.

In the course of this book these tensions are teased into consciousness. Collective contradictions can be helped to shift toward a livable complexity. Only as the duplicity of our theopolitical oxymoron—the imperial messiah—comes into the open does its doubleness yield to dialogue. Negotiation based on dialogue enables responsibility: the ability to respond to our actual worlds. For those worlds, whether enfolded in our religious communities or our neighborhoods, our intellectual aspirations or our political agendas, are comprised of a complexity that is now planetary in its reach. That width intensifies the subterranean life of our collective dreams and nightmares. If it is not too self-serving for a theologian to claim, and even if it is, let me say that I think no one can manage this complexity *responsibly* without some version of spiritual community and commitment.

Politics, however garishly superficial it may seem, always has a depth-dimension. To ignore this matrix of our collective dreams and fears is only to leave its power to ever more frightening manipulations. And it leaves us as individuals disconnected from our interlinkages with each other and with the planet. Thus dissociated, we drift from political despair into a depressive individualism. Consumed by the day-to-day needs and greeds of our private lives (and they are pressured lives indeed), we shrink spiritually, cut off from the planetary openness and flow of creaturely existence. People of faith are only

somewhat less prone to this shrinkage. For a pattern of spiritual individualism—"just me 'n' my Jesus"—pervades religion in the United
States, mingling strangely with the fantasies of collective judgment.
But of course the religious traditions, and in a specific way the biblical ones, can and do also offer a heartier way of interconnection—of
being "members one of another"—and thus a potential at once more
responsible and more profound.

This book comprises a series of theopolitical investigations, a journey into the depth-dimension of our shared national life. The better
to address a particular historical moment, they resist the flight into a
more abstract generality. But the "moment" is not bounded; it refracts
light bouncing from the future back to the beginning and forward
again. These occasional writings succeed my earlier *Apocalypse Now
and Then*; they apply but do not presuppose its analysis. They continue
its advocacy of a "counter-apocalypse," which finds relevance in apocalyptic narrative without acquiescing in its cruelties or its literalizations.
They do not need to be read in any particular sequence; indeed they
enact by their diversity of styles, moods, and strategies a version of
the theopolitical pluralism they advocate. Their present constellation
traces an embracing spiritual perspective, or rather process. It cannot
be read, however, as a comprehensive political theology or a systematic study of messianic imperialism. Many crucial themes remain fragmentary or suggestive. Its argument unfolds in three parts.

The first, "The United States of Apocalypse," raises the question of
God and power in terms of our situation as an imperial superpower.
Chapter 1, "The Armageddon of 9/11," frames the question in terms
of a determinative event, tracing the crisscrossing operations of apocalypticism—Islamic and Christian, terrorist, imperialist, and progressive—that continue to shape our future. Then with Calvin's help I
examine the worship of power itself. Does the very doctrine of omnipotence offer legitimacy to empire? Eerily, Reinhold Niebuhr warned
half a century ago that the peculiar Protestantism of the United States,
which invests our power with innocence, might undermine democracy
and threaten the planet with "defensive war."

In the second part, "Of Beasts and Whores," I probe the apocalyptic
heritage at once more critically and more creatively. A counter-apocalyptic reading here begins to discover the shady figures of apocalypse
costumed for current politics: the white warrior, the great whore, the
quartet of creatures covered with eyes. This optic plurality prophesies

a pluralist and so, in a certain sense, postmodern strategy of interpretation. Examining our political unconscious through these biblical symbols engages feminist, liberation, ecological, and deconstructive hermeneutics. Intriguingly, the tensions among these interpretive perspectives open up—dis/close—a constructive theopolitical space.

Finally, the chapters travel from meditations on the End to the possibilities of Beginning—again. In order to begin to construct a political theology within the complex space of postmodernity, what is called "postcolonial theory," with its particular gift for the "interstitial perspective," the space *between* boundaries, offers a fresh resource. Always between-times, Christian theology here works to come to terms with its own chronic imperial condition. It does not pretend to transcend its global space. It practices an alternative creativity within the interstices of empire. Apocalypse itself recapitulates the Creation. "I am the Alpha and the Omega." *Endzeit gleicht Urzeit.* The New Creation may emulate a unilateral creation from nothing—or a nonlinear creativity from chaos. I abbreviate here the argument of my *Face of the Deep* to invoke the radical relationality from which we may construct, within the chaotic potentiality of democracy, a coalitional politics of love.

But such a counter-imperial theopolitics rests, as we shall see, upon a *theopoetics*. Its justice is not the work of any absolute truth or goodness, for any justice that inflicts apocalyptic literalism on its world produces not a new Jerusalem, but a merciless judgment. We in America have nonetheless never ceased to be blessed; nor have our enemies of the moment. The gospel—unlike the Apocalypse—is unambiguously amorous on this score: God makes the sun to rise on the evil and the good, sends rain on the righteous and on the unrighteous (Matt. 5:45). Within the force field of this love, what is our responsibility?

PART ONE

THE UNITED STATES OF APOCALYPSE

Mapping
Our
Situation

1

The Armageddon of 9/11:
Lament for the New Millennium

Hallelujah. The smoke goes up from her forever and ever.
—Revelation 19:3

The wind is blowing north. As I step out on my twentieth-floor balcony for a breath of sunny autumn stimulation, two months after and ninety blocks north, I am startled to smell it again: that unmistakable, acrid aroma of roasted chemicals. "The smoke of her burning." Nothing collapses distance like the sense of smell. This "she" of Revelations 18 and 19—the great city, her people, her "flutists and trumpeters," her "artisans," her "merchants" who "were the magnates of the earth," the struggling, many-hued workers, the pale proud elite, those who died, those who live—I breathe them in as I write. "Alas, alas, the great city." (November 2001)

Pardon my apocalypse. But bear with it. It is not my own.

Apocalypse is going around. As though on cue, we enact a motif, a vignette, a fragment of its narrative: Christian, Jewish, Muslim, and secular. Apocalypse has been cycling through for centuries. But still, if one doesn't happen to be some sort of fundamentalist, it is not often that one can quote its primary text with such immediacy:

> Alas, alas, the great city,
>   clothed in fine linen,
>   in purple and scarlet,
>   adorned with gold,

3

with jewels, and with pearls!
For in one hour all this wealth has been laid waste!
(Rev. 18:16-17)

In the wake of that single hour a global economy, long wasteful of the earth and its poor, shuddered portentously. And consider the fourth seal—the pale horse, sickly green, whose "rider's name was Death, and Hades followed with him; they were given authority over a fourth of the earth, to kill with sword, famine, and pestilence." (6:8). So the United States claimed military authority over the far reaches of the earth. Famine threatened Afghanistan; the pestilence of anthrax filtered (all too *liter*ally, Latin: "of the letter") through our letters. A plane fell from the New York sky. Osama "I love death" bin Laden announced his capacity to release the nuclear horse. With theatrical flair Manhattan even performed a very rare earthquake. A good moment for religious literalists!

The amplifying feedback loop of dread continues years later to encircle the planet. Because the religious right will also continue to exploit the anxiety, it is crucial that people of a more honest faith not abandon the Apocalypse to the fundamentalists. We too must face and name the mythic scale, the planetary drama, of such a moment. Those of us who do not pretend to read the present off the surface of the Bible have all the more responsibility to read—*theologically* if not literally—the "signs of the times." How else shall we discern within the fluctuations of fear, aggression, and denial an alternative frequency, a pulsation of hope? Hope for us may precisely *not* be about a final omnipotent intervention from above. It may rather inspire a just and sustainable peace process. For now, we are in a war process, a "war on terror" unlike any before in its strangely boundless unpredictability— and so paradoxically more open to the phantasmagoria of apocalyptic prediction. The literal script pushes toward total war: only then, in the end, comes the *pax apocalyptica*. A literalizing apocalypse does not reflect on ancient prophesy—it tries to act it out. It may take secular form as well as religious. Thus, as Edward Said commented a week after 9/11, we are left with gimmicks like "the clash of civilizations" or "Islam versus the West"—"better for reinforcing defensive self-pride than for critical understanding of the bewildering interdependence of our time."[1] These absolute contrasts demonize the opposition; they thus enact an ancient, ever-available script.

A counter-apocalypse suggests another reading of the script of apocalypse. It recognizes that we are within the force field of the narrative, and so it confronts from *within* the self-realizing prophecies of Armageddon.[2] It faces them in order to make them conscious, to disarm their dangerous oblivion, to make peace in whatever piecemeal fashion is possible, already and always. Christians have two strong traditions of response to war: the pacifism of the early Christian community, in which John's apocalypse formed, and the just war doctrine, which evolved as an ideal of constraint for the subsequent Christian empires. Both are problematic: pacifism tends to settle for an unjust peace, but a just peace is as difficult to achieve as a just war. I leave more abstract discussion of these ethical options aside; instead, I want to locate the present configuration within a micro-history of apocalypse. Nothing defuses the high-strung dualism of apocalypse like history itself. For in the history of the last two millennia, we witness not apocalyptic light versus demonic darkness so much as one messianic force projecting darkness onto another, which does likewise. The apocalyptic absolutes clash with each other in religious and secular struggle—and so the absolutes relativize each other.

Islam and Apocalypse

The terrorists framed the United States, long-time Great Satan of Islamic fundamentalism, as the primary cause of Muslim suffering, humiliation, and division. Targeting the economic power stacked in the Twin Towers, they enacted an apocalyptic judgment on "the great whore" of obscene greed. Yet the representatives of Al Qaeda have not even hinted at an economic analysis or strategy. However one parses their motives, they embrace death as martyrs in an ultimate war of pure good versus pure evil. Hence their stunning achievement has inspired—even from a sober, progressive commentator, to whom we will return—the label "apocalyptic terrorism." They represent the most extreme production so far in history of what is called, for lack of a better term, Muslim fundamentalism.[3]

What about the apocalypticism of Islam, however? Certainly in its Christian forms, fundamentalism is by definition apocalyptic, oriented to a final confrontation of absolute good and absolute evil, privileging martyrs among the saved, and bringing the world as we know it to an end. But the sort of literalism that characterizes fundamentalist exegesis is foreign to the elliptical poetry of the Qur'an itself and to the highly evolved disciplines of its interpretive traditions, at least as late and foreign as premillennialist dispensationalism is to its Christian sources. As within the Christian Bible, the apocalyptic symbolism of a final judgment of the just and the unjust pervades the Qur'an. Indeed its discourse of doom emits resonances as potent as those of John's Revelation. Yet Islam eschews the sort of timeline of creation-to-apocalypse that developed early within Christianity and drives toward historical realization. "The Koran is not like the Bible, historical, running from Genesis to Apocalypse," writes Norman O. Brown in appreciation. "The Koran is altogether apocalyptic. The Koran backs off from that linear organization of time, revelation, and history which became the backbone of orthodox Christianity, and remains the backbone of Western culture."[4]

Permit me to cite a bit of Sura 70, not that it "translates," not that I could interpret it, but to give a taste of the Quranic apocalypse. As in every passage of the Qur'an, "Allah, the Merciful, the Compassionate" is the one who speaks:

> Upon the day when heaven shall be as molten copper
> and the mountains shall be as plucked wool-tufts,
> no loyal friend shall question loyal friend. . . .
> Nay verily it is a furnace
> snatching away the scalp,
> calling him who drew back and turned away,
> who amassed and hoarded.
>
> Surely man was created fretful,
> when evil visits him impatient,
> when good visits him, grudging,
> save those that pray,
> and continue at their prayers,
> those in whose wealth is a right known
> for the beggar and the outcast,
> who confirm the Day of Doom
> and go in fear of the chastisement of the Lord. . . .
> And guard their private parts
> save from their wives and what their right hand owns
> then not being blameworthy. . . .
> Those shall be in gardens, high-honored.[5]

As in biblical prophecy, economic injustice figures prominently as doom-worthy; what counts as virtue in capitalism—amassing wealth— is a supreme vice. Likewise, both traditions feature the attempt to contain sexuality, male as well as female, within an intensified patri-archal propriety. Moreover, as in the Bible, the Day of Doom comes at no predictable point, no end of a line: "To Allah belong the secrets of the heavens and the earth, and the matter of the Hour is as the twinkling of an eye, or it is nearer still."[6] Also both books remain consistent as to the *agency* of final judgment: the punishment of the evildoer is a divine prerogative—"so their Lord crushed them for their sin, and levelled them." Such punishment is *not* to be exercised by Allah's followers. "Surely upon Us rests the guidance, and to Us belong the Last and the First. No, I have warned you of a Fire that flames."

Islam and Modernity

Deep dissatisfaction with historical injustice boils throughout the prophetic traditions, usually demanding not Armageddon but active application to human social orders. Indeed Mohammed himself (unlike Jesus, who did not live long enough) conducted a wondrously successful experiment in socially just, spiritually attuned living during his last ten years of life in al-Medina.[7] That memory and its texts give rise in Islam—more consistently than in Christianity, which tended to postpone justice until final judgment—to endless attempts to bring about social justice within human political forms. The concern for the poor, the widow, the orphan, never falls silent in the Qur'an. The *zakat*, or "alms tax," is the third of the five pillars of Islam, to be paid every year to help the poor.[8] The stunning success of Islam within one century of the prophet's death—into an empire extending through northern Africa, the Spanish Pyrenees, and the Himalayas—was the product of both religious energy and pragmatic expansion. "Western people often assume that Islam is a violent, militaristic faith which imposed itself on its subject peoples at sword-point. This is an inac-curate interpretation of the Muslim wars of expansion."[9] Its success must also be attributed to its relatively moderate practices, requiring obedience to its laws but not conversion to its religion. The conquer-ing Arabs often were met with little resistance.[10]

For almost a millennium medieval Muslim empires hugely sur-
passed Western European achievements in trade, social organization,
and military conquest. But through what we call the birth of the modern nation state, beginning in Spain five hundred years ago, with its
ethnic cleansing (the mass expulsion of Jews and the Muslim Moors)
and its aggressive colonial drive, Europe reinvented itself.[11] But only
two centuries ago did the tables of power turn: first with the British
colonization of Moghul India, in the economic plundering and political domination of Muslim Bengal. Then in 1798 Napoleon, admirer of
both the European crusaders and Islam, attacked Egypt brutally and
efficiently.[12] Scientists, Orientalists, and an Enlightenment ideology of
freedom accompanied his modern occupation army. The Muslim world
naturally mutated in response to wave after wave of the aggressions
of western modernity. Muslim leaders had little choice but to mod-
ernize in self-defense. They follow the example of Mehmet Ali, who
responded to the encounter with Napoleon by seizing power in Egypt
in 1805 and superimposing a European-style, secularizing modernity.[13]
The ruthless impositions of these alien forms on local cultures—both
by regional leaders and by Europeans—were profoundly disorienting.
Modernization was experienced by many Muslims as its own day of
doom: "major battles; formidable happenings; calamitous occurrences;
terrible catastrophes; the multiplication of evils, . . . the disruption of
time, the inversion of the natural order."[14] The modernization process
systematically targeted Muslim traditions and institutions, portrayed
by indigenous and colonial leaders as obstacles to progress.

Islamic protest movements arose. Starting in 1929, the Society of
Muslim Brothers—from which hail many Al Qaeda brothers and principles—worked to fill the vacuum. It developed a network of social,
educational, and economic services, Quranically inspired, for the
poor of Egypt. It was too popular to be tolerated by the secular Arab
state and only became a militant underground movement in response
to vicious persecution—especially by the secularizing nationalist
Nasser.[15] A similar process transpired in Iran, under the ruthless secularizing rule of Reza Shah Pahlavi. When clergy and students pro-
tested, he had them murdered. In 1920 the young Ruhollah Musavi
Kohmeini (1902–1989) came onto the scene, a Shiite mystic, not a
"fundamentalist" until much later. In the aftermath of Reza Shah and
World War II, the United States began to play a new role in the region.
Through a CIA-engineered coup in 1953, the popular and democrat-

ically elected Mussadiq, who had nationalized the oil industry, was replaced by the deposed son of Reza Shah. "For the hundreds of millions of dollars that the American colonialist imperialists will gain in oil, the oppressed nation will lose all hope of liberty and will have a negative opinion about all the Western world."[16]

By necessity the Islamic movements militarized, attempting to defend the integrity of Muslim society, both spiritually and socially. Yet this reaction strains Islam. The ruling Shiite theocracy of Iran, for example, represents a bizarre transmutation of the subtle mysticism and deferred messianism of the Shiite tradition. Fundamentalism began to appear, for instance, in the influential ideology of the Pakistani Nawdudi, who called for a universal jihad against the encroaching western secularism. He argued that "jihad was the central tenet of Islam." As Karen Armstrong comments, "This was an innovation."[17] But only in Sayyid Qutb (1906–1966) did the founder of Islamic fundamentalism in the Sunni world appear. Witnessing Nasser's torture and execution of his fellow Egyptian Brothers, he called for a violent jihad for the political victory of Islam.[18] His innovative Islam provided the main inspiration for the Taliban. That the militant fundamentalisms, contrary to western stereotype, hardly pose a unified picture is suggested by the fact that in the 1990s the Taliban murdered thousands of Shiite Muslims.

Under Reza Shah, who forbade Islamic dress, soldiers tore off women's veils with their bayonets. The veil had become a symbol of the obstacle to progress—a progress understood not as women's equality but as westernization. No wonder many Muslim women voluntarily wear the veil as a symbol of resistance to western cultural dominance.[19] Compare the snapshot today: women's faces bared and smiling on the streets of Kabul. "Apocalypse"—the "unveiling"? Who will give it a single face?

Christian Endtimes

While all fundamentalisms offer return to the true origin of the religion, they can be contextualized only as modern phenomena, that is, as radical reactions against modern aggression. But of the three monotheistic religions, Islam was the last to develop its fundamentalist strain, "when modern culture began to take root in the Muslim world in the late 1960's and 1970's."[20] Unlike Christian fundamentalism, the Muslim analogue stresses the prophetic social justice tradition. It must defend against the economic and military aggressions as well as the secularism of western modernity. The point is that if we want to understand rather than demonize all who resonate with Al Qaeda, we will have to understand ourselves better. And we "ourselves" are also partly constituted by the tensions of modern secularization and fundamentalist reaction. I cannot detail this more familiar history here but only point to a peculiar symmetry.

Our own fundamentalists sound strangely like "theirs." Instantaneous was Jerry Falwell's response to 9/11: He said he would point a figurative finger at those "who have tried to secularize America" and say, "You helped this happen." It is the feminists, "abortionists," homosexuals, and defenders of civil liberties who got the finger. Added Pat Robertson, "I totally concur." Yet they are loathe to identify God with the cause of Islamic terror. So "He" didn't directly will it. "He lifted the curtain of protection."[21] Yet another "unveiling"! Thus the United States, with its sinful secularism, attested to flagrantly in gender equality and sexual immorality, is getting its comeuppance. Christian and Muslim absolutists are one in blaming secular America for 9/11.

A more moderate fundamentalist approach, intent on displaying its patriotism, runs like this. "Colin Powell said it well, 'We will go after the branch and root to get at these terrorists.' For it is the soil that yields the plant. If it is Osama bin Laden, he can only exist as an evil terrorist because of the country that harbored and supported him." The writer takes Powell's justification of a war against Afghanistan and turns it into a call for our repentance: "As Christians, it is also now our job to go after the branch and root as well, and even to the soil, to create the kind of environment that will please God for the fruit that will be produced. In our own country, we have not done that well. The devastation of these days is a wake up call."[22] I would concur, as would most progressive commentators, with that latter point. After much biblical prooftexting, she gets down to her point: no call to deal justly with Islamic peoples or our own ethnically vulnerable populations, but rather the familiar agenda to correct all of our sexual deviancies "so that we don't become like them!" The author fails to note that her problem with secularism echoes "theirs," that the Taliban's sexual ethos resembles her own ideal (except that "she" can speak of it). The main difference among fundamentalisms (apart from the divinization of a prophet as God) seems to be the lack of interest in economic and social injustice among the born-again.

However much we oppose their agendas—and certainly their violence—shall we scorn the anti-secularist apocalypses? If the modern destruction of communities and their traditional belief patterns has yielded awesome technology and some precious rights, its proud constructions do not bridge the spiritual void or the widening gaps between the affluent and the destitute. That project has won its indubitable progress in science, standard of life, democracy, and finally even the rights of women at unbearable cost: repeated acts of ethnic cleansing, conquest, and genocide and an economic hegemony that keeps most of the world's populations, human and nonhuman, dependent and subject to our markets and if need be to extinction. So the hope for a just and sustainable peace arises within a theological *post*modernism, predicated on a steadfast excavation of the systematic violence of the modern project of the last five hundred years.[23]

Is the whole modern complex fatally flawed? Should the apocalyptic reverberations of that question be ignored just now? Neither Christian nor Islamic fundamentalists will join the (too secular) struggle of environmentalists and workers against globalization. But they all know how to map the economy of the Beast. While always locating Armageddon in the Middle East, U.S. fundamentalists have long identified Manhattan as Babylon: "The nations have drunk of the wine of the wrath of her fornication, . . . and the merchants of the earth have grown rich from the power of her luxury" (Rev. 18:3). Even this feminist pro-choice New Yorker unhappily appreciates the fit.

The Empire Strikes Back

In Christianity the prophetic social-justice tradition, along with its anti-imperialist apocalypse, was marginalized from the time of the Christianization of the Roman Empire. The United States is today's only candidate for world empire; more specifically, what is dubbed our "economic neo-imperialism," with the backup of our military hyper-technology, maintains our global dominance. Apocalypse in the biblical text and in the 9/11 strike is directed *against* Rome (Babylon), against all empire. Of course the empire strikes back. Our government sends forth the powers of state-authorized terror, legalized as war. But being the government of a nation born and born again from the narratives of millennialist messianism, it cannot resist the rhetoric of apocalypse: our mission, our moment; "they" are evil; we fight pure evil; if our bombs cause "collateral damage," that too is the enemy's fault for hiding behind women and children; if children starve there, if freedom is compromised here, that is too bad; we will not stop until evil has been annihilated. Yet if our aggression only spawns martyrs for Islam, does this mean that we will never stop, that this final war will spiral on—until the End?

The logic of apocalyptic overdetermination need not prevail. The "spiral of violence" can be broken.[24] But we may have a difficult time imagining a realistic alternative. The unknowable gains daily in end-time density: How will our "defensive" aggressions produce security and not endless war? Might the terrorists get nuclear weapons? small-pox? How can our assault fail to unify more Muslims against us, Israel, and their own hated governments? Will all the issues that matter unconditionally to the future of a sustainable planet, such as global warming, the ozone hole, the economy, racial justice, AIDS, educa-tion—already on the back burner—be ignored until truly it is too late? The uncertainty lurches at moments toward the unbearable. Yet it is the tone of *certainty* that rings apocalyptic: the certainty of what is evil—and so of "our" goodness. Fundamentalism has reacted not only against the arrogance of modernity but against its growth toward pluralism, ambiguity, indeterminacy. Yet who does not grasp at straws of certainty when so much is at risk?

Left Apocalypse

Even the progressive U.S. response gets caught in the apocalyptic mir-ror-game. Chickens come home to roost: the *real* cause is our policy in the Middle East, especially Israel, or the *real* cause is the global economy. While I heard myself in the initial shock laying these propo-sitions on my students, and heard them echoing through my theo-logical community, their indignant certainties rang hollow at ground zero. I needed something more difficult and honest than the mono-causal explanations, the warmed-over and misfitting Vietnam-era slo-gans, the I-told-you-so's that did not.[25] The construal of Islam as a mere third-world victim of an omnipotent United States suggests a kind of negative grandiosity that may satisfy our conventions of protest but ill serves its own cause—that of peace with justice. This is not just because it is heard as "justifying" the terrorists, but because it also reinscribes the Orientalist stereotype of the helpless, feminized, and dangerously homogenized Other. Moreover it reduces the long history of aggressive interactions between Islamic empires and the crusading powers of the west, as well as the history of internecine battles within Islam itself, to a faded leftist messianism: evil United States versus oppressed innocence.

Might we instead confess that the United States has been multiply culpable in the Middle East: in donning during the Cold War the old mantle of the European imperial aggressions; in our economically determinative, ecologically devastating oil addiction; in our support of the Israeli state's immoral policies toward the Palestinians; in our patronage of unpopular Arab governments. These legitimate grievances against us ferment a bitter, transgenerational rage—rife for manipulation by propagandists and terrorists. But they do not collapse into a single explanation of 9/11. Indeed the very model of a monocausal explanation, with its linear predictability and its indignant certainty, echoes with the hoofbeats of secular apocalypse.

A nonlinear model will better serve understanding. It requires multiple causal paths, many but not all derived from U.S. neo-imperialism. These paths wind through the oldest internecine minefield of the Middle East, and therefore of western civilization: that of the sibling rivals of the patrilineage of Abraham. In other words there are multiple causes that at every juncture require a complex analysis. For us to take *responsibility* for our own arrogant and unjust history in the Middle East is not to accept *blame* for the terrorist attack. We did not "cause" it. We can acknowledge that we have done much to make such an attack likely and that until we shift course in policies vastly exceeding the matter of our own security but essential to it, we will continue to lend terrorism a wide base of respect among Muslims of many perspectives. *Responsible action* is based on continued work to understand and thus *respond* to—not just *react* to—those who act as our enemies. A strategy of responsible action would not grant moral credibility to terrorists; on the contrary, it would be the only way to maintain moral credibility for the United States among our allies and at home.

Love Whom?

For a U.S. Christian leader at this moment, apocalyptic certainty—with its aura of political purity—is not only unnecessary but illusory. This much seems clear to me, however: we must make clear that all rhetoric of Christian virtue or heritage is disqualified if we do not espouse a Christian view of the enemy. Does this mean, for example, to "love" Osama? "Love the enemy" was an imperative of the gospel, not the apocalypse. It has held up poorly under the least historic pressure. It may never have been directed toward national or political enemies anyway. Perhaps for this reason we better keep trying it: on an interdependent and indeterminate planet it may be the path of greatest realism. But the love imperative does not call me to *feel* love for any mass murderer. It does not imagine reconciliation with active terrorists. I do not believe it calls me to "forgive" anyone who does not want to be forgiven. Fullness of forgiveness is impossible apart from repentance, that is, cessation of hostility. But a certain initiation of forgiveness acknowledges the potentiality for change: it loves the other in their potentiality for love. I love that potentiality in any terrorist, in any warrior, in any human. And of course these "others" are routinely sacrificing their lives for their own version of a great love. We can recognize love even in its worst deformations. I love it as a potentiality for peace, even as I love my own potentiality to outgrow fear and respond in love. This love does not work in a modern, therefore sentimentalized, individualized, and quite unbiblical sense. The inscrutably all-embracing, equal-opportunity love of God keeps on falling like the rain, shining like the sun. That God exacts from the followers of Jesus—the Jewish radical, prophet among Muslims, incarnation of Love itself among Christians—at least some version of the golden rule.

We must demand from any Christians, even a smugly born-again president, what Islam also demands of its followers: that *we treat all enemies as human beings, that is, as creatures capable of responsibility and only therefore culpable.* We hold them responsible for their inhumanities precisely because we are willing to take responsibility for our own. The Christian principle does not read: do unto others what they would do unto us. Their violence against noncombatants will never justify ours. Their ethnocentrism, hatred, or aggression no more justifies our own than our own prior ethnocentrism, hatred, and aggression have justified theirs. Rather it is only our adherence to a just standard that justifies our condemnation of their violence. And *justice* means *acting in consciousness of the relationships that bind us together, relations of fragile, global interdependence.*

Such an interdependence expresses the nonlinear, multicausal history that binds us all and that can amplify chaotically out of control at any time. The responsible answer to chaos, however, is not dominance but wisdom. Uncertainty will not go away. But our fear of the others with whom we are globally interdependent could dissipate. For it is our interdependence—even of "Islam" and "the west," "Christian" and "secular"—that can, and for Christians must, reveal the difficult universality of divine love.

This is not Sunday school. This is the world hanging, as it sometimes does, in the balance. Concretely: responsibility to ourselves and to the world dictates that we recognize our specific interdependence with the Muslim peoples. Responsibility would also mean a persistent renegotiation of the terms of our alliance with Israel. Israel has been a comfortable, western-style ally; but Israel's own secular modernism, a thorn in the flesh of embattled Islam, is ironically belied by the fundamentalist messianism of its growing ultraorthodox constituency. Christians must step back from the apocalyptic mirror-game of the new Muslim anti-Semitism and the Israeli anti-Palestinianism.

Religious leaders in this century must insist upon *at least* a tri-faith, nonlinear model for peacemaking. We do this confessing our part in the "many-sided contest among these three followers—not one of them by any means a monolithic, unified camp—of the most jealous of all gods."[26] We must insist upon the participation of the daughters of Sarah and of Hagar at every negotiating table. How else should the fratricide cease? We support the goal not of the "end" of terrorism, let alone the empire of the United States, but of "the healing of the nations" (Rev. 22:2). History remains, however anxiously, open. We decode the Alpha and the Omega not as the pretext for a final war but the open text of a counter-apocalypse.

———

My cab is stuck in heavy evening traffic (too many of us afraid of subways this month). Fortunately the driver is an interesting man, articulate and kind. He plunges right in: "Of course we must make someone pay for the attack. But the bombs won't do it. We can't ignore everything else, especially the economy. He says he'd been a Marine in Vietnam, and he recognizes the quagmire we are quickly sinking into. He says he was drafted, and he should have taken his father's advice and resisted or fled to Canada. He fears that our president is a "religious fanatic." He tells me of customers rehearsing the newly relevant verses of Nostradamus. After we have stopped and I have paid, he turns his full face to me, handsome and black. He says he does not want to depress me. But the aurora up by the Eskimos has been brilliantly red this month. This only happens before terrible world crisis. And the Bible refers to the two towers. He says, this war may really be the beginning of the end. You know, the End of Time.

I have so liked this thoughtful cabbie. I cannot just shake or nod my head condescendingly. "Don't you think the apocalypse could be a warning, not a foregone conclusion?" I ask him. "It may not have anything to do with our response," he says. "It may be a matter of forces we have no control over." "Yes. But you seem to live like such a free person, you think hard, you make responsible choices. What if God is the one who inspires that freedom, not the one who works us like puppets?" He laughs out loud—"You may be right." He drives off chuckling to himself. I stand in the darkness for a moment. I am grateful for the uncertainty.

In the name of God, the Merciful, the Compassionate.

2

Preemption and Omnipotence:
A Niebuhrian Prophecy

> We might be tempted to bring the whole of modern history to a tragic conclusion by one final and mighty effort to overcome its frustrations. The political term for such an effort is "preventive war."
>
> —Reinhold Niebuhr, *The Irony of American History*

The explosion of 9/11 produced a vast cloud of opportunity. Some were sure that the Middle Eastern turbulence of the endtimes had finally begun, with rapture sure to follow. For others, "the New Pearl Harbor" provided the long-awaited opportunity to push for a global military hegemony that could stabilize the world. We got neither the Messiah nor the stability. Instead, we got a full-blown American Empire—a phrase that at the turn of the century still seemed like old leftist rhetoric seeking its own opportunities. At this point it is up to liberal and progressive religious leaders to make another use of the "opportunity": not to proliferate homiletically overheated denunciations, but to expose *theologically* the idolatry of U.S. global pretensions. These pretensions oscillate between the military face of empire, emboldened by 9/11—and the incessant voracity of its smoother, bipartisan economic face. And while U.S. regimes and strategies shift, the political cloud released by 9/11 may take much of the new century to dissipate. If we do not trace the imperial identity that revealed itself amid "the smoke of her burning," the odor does threaten to "go up from her forever and ever."

Innocence and Power

The United States does not refer to itself as an empire, since it lacks a monarchy. In other words, we do have elections (more or less) and not dynasties (well, not exactly). Old issues echo in the terminological question of an "American Empire." Until the Civil War the concept of an American Empire was commonplace. George Washington and Ben Franklin routinely referred to the United States as a "rising empire." While "legend and tradition require that the American Republic appear anti-monarchical and anti-imperial," according to a historian writing half a century ago, the executive power belies this "legend of the Revolution."[1] But under the Bush Jr. regime, our officials learned not to mince words anymore. They began to refer to our "hegemonic unipolarity" and our "appropriate global dominance." That dominance was carved into imperial marble for the twenty-first century with the declaration of our right to use overwhelming military force preemptively whenever we want.[2] As the chapters in Part I of this volume show, however, the question is not *whether* America is an empire but only *what kind.*

This situation cannot simply be voted out of office. With a different administration, our global domination might be exercised with a greater sense of responsibility. But the imperial configuration will not soon dissipate. So it is time to raise theological questions about *power*—and to question theological answers. No great empires have been lacking in religious justifications for their apparently irresistible powers of expansion. What makes us special? Not long before his death, Edward Said stated, "The difference between America and the classic empires of the past is that, even though each empire asserted its utter originality and its determination not to repeat the overreaching ambitions of imperial predecessors, this one does so with an astonishing affirmation of its nearly sacrosanct altruism and well-meaning innocence."[3]

Americans ask: "How can they hate *us*? Maybe we're not sophisticated like old Europe, maybe we slip up here and there (a few bad apples), but don't they see our innocent, exuberant, have-a-nice-day goodness?" This aura of sacrosanct, youthful power, which has always distinguished our imperialism, requires theological decoding. A halo of unquestionability surrounds the literally boundless aggression of neoliberal economic globalization and now also our military super-power, redefined by its policy of preemptive war. We cannot read this halo only historically or politically. It is not a mere laurel wreath, suited to a Roman god. It is alive and vibrating with theological information. Our "manifest destiny"—manifest first upon contiguous lands and then, a century ago, across the seas—has always bristled with Christian power codes. Theology may be an important inside agent in breaking codes and also in *transcoding*: translating the codes into alternative contexts of communication. Let us try to *transcode* the spiritual politics of power.

Theology has an internal tradition of resistance to U.S. imperialism. Half a century ago Reinhold Niebuhr wrote: "We have been so deluded by the concept of our innocency that we are ill prepared to deal with the temptations of power which now assail us."[4] He thought that we had heretofore oscillated between isolationism, which means to ignore our responsibilities to the other nations, and imperialism, which means "to dominate them by our power." At the dawn of the nuclear age and in the aftermath of the Second World War, the discourse of our messianic innocence was just beginning to pose its apocalyptic threat to the world. Niebuhr investigated both the Puritan and the Jeffersonian sources of our delusion of innocence—a paradoxically very uncalvinist delusion—that "we had been called out by God to create a new humanity. We were God's new Israel."[5] Niebuhr knew we would not soon forfeit our power. He called not for some new, revolutionary myth of innocence, but for a humbling sense of irony in the face of our self-contradictions. Half a century later, still protesting our innocence, we are if anything even less able to discern a third way, a way of globally democratic multilateralism. In the face of our long history of domination encrypted with faith, we have failed to learn the Niebuhrian irony. Instead we are far better armed technologically, economically, and, I fear, religiously. Absolute power is treated not as absolute corruption—not even as temptation—but as blessing.

Apocalypse and Imperial Legitimation

Hannah Arendt has argued that *violence* is instrumental and hence requires only *justification*: an end justifies the means. *Power*, by contrast, requires *legitimation*, which comes from stories of creation—of beginning and new beginning. Religion within our secular empire has provided covert legitimation: The enemy is not merely a historical foe, but a diabolical dark force against which only the white light of our messianic goodness can prevail. Over and over we have heard that "America will call evil by its name." The name of the Beast? But religion has also offered *overt* legitimacy: we heard from President Bush that "the liberty we prize is not America's gift to the world, it is God's gift to humanity." (So it was God's gift we brought to Iraq.) "There's *power, wonder-working power*, in the goodness and idealism and faith of the American people."[6] The quotation from an evangelical hymn invests our national innocence with divine power. The irony seems to have escaped the fundamentalist public: that the hymn refers to the blood of "the lamb" slaughtered by the imperial superpower of his day. Indeed, according to the Book of Revelation, the most misused text of all, the name of the Beast is none other than the name of the dominant empire of the time, which was then Rome. The Apocalypse is a parable of terror, transcoding the blowback that brings down every human empire.[7]

It is tempting to take up a righteous apocalyptic stance of anti-imperialism. However, within its Northern Hemisphere context at least, the church will do better with counter-imperialism, along with an honest dose of Niebuhrian irony, for Christianity long ago lost its innocence. It lost it to empire itself, at the point of the Constantinian conversion of the empire to Christianity. "When the Western world accepted Christianity," wrote Alfred North Whitehead a decade after World War I, "Caesar conquered; and the received text of Western theology was edited by his lawyers. . . . The brief Galilean vision of humility flickered throughout the ages, uncertainly."[8]

Or did the loss of innocence begin earlier, even in the anti-empire of the vision of apocalypse, when it mirrors and mimics the empire—with a panorama of messianic armies, holy genocide, divine ecocide, and all penetrating divine power? The apocalyptic codes have routinely justified empire as well as anti-empire. The Crusades were experienced as apocalypse come true—forty thousand Muslim women, children, and men were slaughtered in two days in Jerusalem. An eyewitness, rendering history as a paraphrase of Rev. 15:20, wrote rapturously of the wonderful sights to be seen: "In the Temple and porch of Solomon, men rode in blood up to their knees and bridle reins. Indeed it was a just and splendid judgment of God that this place should be filled with the blood of the unbelievers."[9] If, as Rahul Mahajan argues, America's "War on Terrorism" has unleashed a "new crusade," with a "new rhetoric of justification," the religious code remains indispensable. As Mahajan says, "No government, whether dictatorship or democracy, can remain in power if it cannot represent its actions and ultimately its authority as legitimate."[10]

But our global hegemony has drawn its aura of sacrality not only from the warring *apocalyptic* extremities it requires. We model ourselves less after the crusaders than after the British Empire. Its Protestantism was constrained and decidedly nonapocalyptic. Richard Hakluyt, a scholar writing in 1589, during the reign of Queen Elizabeth I, argued that if the Pope could give Ferdinand and Isabella the right to occupy "such island and lands as you may have discovered or are about to discover" outside Christendom, the English crown had a duty to enlarge and advance the faith of Christ "on behalf of Protestantism."[11] Protestantism enabled Britain to advance from mere piracy against the religiously legitimated Spanish holdings to an empire of its own. Modernity, it seems, required wave after wave of conquest for Christ.

The main problem, however, is not a past Christian loss of innocence. It is rather the persistent delusion of innocence. And yet there have always been some Christians who wake up and "come of age," in Bonhoeffer's sense. Christianity within its waves of influence does not only legitimate but also vehemently *withholds* legitimacy, as when Bishop de las Casas denounced the brutality of his fellow Spaniards in their "New World." Or it deploys its influence for justice, as with the church-based British grassroots campaign that brought about the abolishment of slavery in 1806. But this great evangelical achievement was not a work of mere innocence: Using the same logic—that not only whites are fully human before God—the same group (Clapham Commons) broke through the rigid British constraint on missionary activity in India. This group did not question the British Empire but made it a tool of Christian mission, leading quite directly to a new Indian sense of cultural violation, to the Indian Army mutiny, and thereby to the barbaric British reprisals.

Such ambiguities do not *delegitimate* Christianity. They simply display its capacity for both self-righteous idolatry and prophetic iconoclasm. It is *because* the church is implicated in empire that we can decode and transcode the idolatries of empire. Of course, the legitimating master code is not reducible to religion. It is heavily shaped by the secular rhetoric of "democracy" and "freedom" as well. But these appeals lack circumstantial credibility and, for many Americans, ultimacy. They have to be shored up by apocalyptic, inherently anti-democratic signals. *Legitimation* in its appeal to ultimacy is bigger than instrumental *justification.* Both are different from *explanation*, which gives reasons. There are several likely *explanations* for the post-9/11 empire. I will list nine: (1) plain fear, manipulated to include the Arab and the Muslim in general; (2) an almost audible sigh of relief at having finally found an enemy worthy to fill the void left by the communist Other; (3) the felt virility of this identity, its explosion of potency putting behind us the long-haired Vietnam wimp-out; (4) our relation as the New Israel to the Newer or Older or Greater Israel—a state no one calls a wimp; (5) the neoliberal global economy, combined with a reaction against its *de*nationalizing tendencies; (6) the captivity of the U.S. media by monopoly capitalism; (7) the stupefaction of the public and reduction of the U.S. attention span to the size of an ahistorical sound bite; (8) the production not of engaged citizens but of docile consumers who, after bouts of apocalyptic excitement, retreat into the comfort of expensive addictions, oil foremost; (9) the lack of effective cosmopolitan governance of a postmodern, ecologically interdependent globe of high speed communications and weapons technology, producing new perils and needs—including no doubt the need for international, cosmopolitan strategies of *responsible* preemptive defense.

All of these explanations are true as far as they go. But they do not add up to a justification. Together they suggest the overdetermination of our imperial condition. Legitimation is always greater than the sum of justifications. So let us direct our attention to the aura that plays about all of these reasons, in a certain sense holding them together. Let us focus on *the halo surrounding our empire*, not just in its deeply embedded Judeo-Christianisms, but also in its hard-line secular state doctrine.

Evil and Idealism

How is it that we as a post-Vietnam people could come to regard military superpower, unilaterally deployed, as *good*? Not just justifiable as necessary violence, but legitimate as a virtue, a force for peace, order, and freedom? The particular justifications disintegrate—Osama, Saddam, weapons of mass destruction. Yet the glow of righteousness persists. It is not only that might *makes* right, but that this might *is* right: manifest destiny, the special providence of America, the city on the hill. "God Bless America"—not to *make* us good, but because we *are* good. The phenomenon is as old as we are, and so Niebuhr's warning—that "we are still inclined to pretend that our power is exercised by a peculiarly virtuous nation"—deserves its near-canonical status.

It is perhaps not surprising, therefore, that this very sentence gets attacked in *The War over Iraq,* a book written to prepare the way for war *with* Iraq. The authors, Lawrence Kaplan and William Kristol of the Project for the New American Century, (correctly) accuse Niebuhr and the political realists in general of trying to inhibit "a messianic impulse" that was, in their view, able to "lead America to upset the balance of power between it and the Soviet Union." At *this* point, they argue, "there is something perverse in continuing to doubt the efficacy of promoting democratic change abroad in light of the record of the past three decades."[12] Their examples are telling: "After we have already seen dictatorships toppled by democratic forces in such seemingly unlikely places as the Philippines, Indonesia, Chile, Nicaragua," why stop now? They do not mention that in both Indonesia and Chile the CIA toppled democratic governments, after which the United States supported two of the most brutal military dictatorships of the twentieth century; that in Nicaragua the democratizing forces we equipped and called "freedom fighters" fit our own definition of terrorism; or that the "democracy" in the Philippines is purely formal, being controlled by a tiny plutocracy.[13] On the basis of such grotesque misreadings of history, the hard-nosed secular theorists of the Bush regime, such as Paul Wolfowitz and Richard Perle, espouse "idealism." They unapologetically proclaim the "American Ideal" as *Pax Americana.* But by defending our unilateralism as not only benevolent but as messianic, their Aristotelian-Straussian idealism colludes with the populism of the Christian right, including the president's own evangelical posture, marked by frequent White House prayer meetings. This mixture worked for Ronald Reagan and was reintroduced at a new pitch.

Let me suggest that it is this potent merger of elitist idealism with conservative Christian populism that has provided the overarching legitimation for our empire. It is specifically in the code of *evil,* furthermore, that this idealism fuses with apocalypticism. Thus the phrase "axis of evil" cunningly conflates the "evil empire" denounced by Reagan with "the axis" powers of World War II. The Bush Doctrine, write Kristol and Kaplan, "signals a return to this earlier era, when Munich, not Vietnam, was the cautionary example."[14] They argue, contra Niebuhr, that our temptation is isolationism, not imperialism. But this attempt to restore "the Great Generation" deploys a fundamentalist demonization of the Other not needed in World War II or even the Cold War. Defending Bush from his detractors' "howls of derision" over his use of the term "evil," Kaplan and Kristol insist that "as the events of 9/11 remind us, evil exists in this world, and it has consequences." Who can disagree? But with a great logical somersault, they continue: "Fortunately, evil can be defeated. Just as Ronald Reagan's assault on the 'evil empire' was key to toppling Soviet communism."[15] *This* is cryptotheology. Never mind that *biblically* speaking, evil is *never* simply defeated, at least not in history and not by humans. Evil is often constrained, tricked, or exorcised. Jesus had for instance called the pigs suffering from possession "legion," satirizing the police power of the Roman legions. Evil as such is defeated in the Bible, *if* it is at all, by the final advent of the Messiah. As Niebuhr argued, America's messianic idealism sabotages the development of the political wisdom to know that "powerful forces may be beguiled, deflected, and transmuted but never simply annulled or defied."[16] Whether or not our policies protect us from any evil, they certainly depend parasitically upon its foreign manifestations: without melodramatic figures of evil such as Osama bin Laden and Saddam Hussein, the Bush administration would have continued to founder. As British novelist and commentator Tariq Ali observed, "the leaders of the United States wish to be judged by their choice of enemies rather than the actual state of the world."[17]

Is the aura of morality with which we go forth to "overcome evil" a merely expedient, hypocritical justification—a front for hypercapitalism? I am arguing that it is always a mistake to underestimate the sincerity behind this halo. No matter how many and how profitable the U.S. government's falsehoods, it perpetrates them in the name of a larger truth. For it the halo holds what is called now "our American creed" and the "Bush Doctrine"—the defining feature of which is military preemption—in place. The halo holds together our might with our self-perceived goodness. But what energizes the halo? What legitimating symbolism, what code of creation, provides the energy, if not that of a deity who is at once all-good and all-mighty? So here is the question for theology: Might it be the very doctrine of divine omnipotence that charges the halo with its holy electricity?

Omnipotence and Preemption

What would omnipotence, a dignified doctrine of classical Christianity—and of orthodox Judaism and Islam as well—have to do with any doctrine of imperial human power? If human superpower apes divine power, it is committing the crassest idolatry. If a logic of preemption is gaining legitimacy from a prior logic of omnipotence—or if the U.S. halo is sucking energy from a theological assumption—religious leaders had better take note. To test for this idolatrous displacement, I would like to host a strange conversation between the Bush doctrine idealists and the great idol-smasher John Calvin.

As the process theologian David Griffin has demonstrated, it is Calvin who most forcefully spells out the implications of traditional theism.[18] Calvin confronts head-on the difficult logic of a power that controls all things. He rejects the easy out, common in his day as well as our own, to say that the omnipotent God only *permits,* rather than actually *causes,* evil things to happen. "God does not permit," Calvin thunders back, "but governs by his power." Continuing, he says that "they babble and talk absurdly who, in place of God's Providence, substitute bare permission—as if God sat in a watchtower awaiting chance events, and his judgment thus depended upon human will."[19] Calvin's God, being omnipotent, does not wait for things to happen and then respond.

Do we hear an echo of this doctrine of providence in the doctrine of preemption? The 2002 *National Security Strategy* document states, "Given the goals of rogue states and terrorists, the United States can no longer rely on a reactive posture as we have in the past."[20] Preemption, like predetermination, is proaction, indeed pre-action, not reaction.

That such a teaching makes God responsible for evil as well as good is not a problem for Calvin. What bothers him instead is that "today so many venomous dogs assail this doctrine." Rather familiarly, what matters is to silence the critics, not to examine the merits of their critique. "Paul does not, as do those I have spoken of, labor anxiously to make *false excuses in God's defense*: he only warns that it is unlawful for the clay to quarrel with its potter."[21] Similarly, the new imperialists eschew argument: "A humane future, then, will require an American foreign policy that is *unapologetic, idealistic, assertive and well funded*. America must not only be the world's policeman or its sheriff, it must be its beacon and guide."[22] "The alternative to American leadership," write Kaplan and Kristol, "is a chaotic, Hobbesian world where there is no authority to thwart aggression, ensure peace and security or enforce international norms." In other words, the horrific chaos that our foreign policy has produced is—if you squint patriotically—really *order*; our dominance creates *freedom*; our wars ensure *peace*; and open defiance of half a century of international law enforces "international norms."

Incomprehensible doublespeak? But omnipotence is precisely the doctrine of God's "incomprehensible providence." Calvin courageously acknowledges the horror of double predestination, including the damnation of unbaptized infants—who were damned only "because it so pleased God." Showing a spark of humanity, Calvin continues: "The decree is dreadful indeed, I confess." But, rather than questioning whether such a dreadful decree could have originated with an all-good deity, he simply suggests that we must "tremble at so deep a mystery."[23] The unquestionable assumption is that nothing happens unless God specifically wills it, no matter how horrific. Sometimes God must shock and awe.

What are we to make of this? God's loving goodness and God's omnipotence might seem, in every event of unjust suffering, to contradict each other. By definition, however, God's power and love are one. This traditional unity of attributes becomes a "mystery"—a euphemism for contradiction—only if the divine power is, with Calvin, understood to be all-controlling. He recognizes the ethical consequences: "When we are *unjustly* wounded by men, let us overlook their wickedness (which would but worsen our pain and sharpen our minds to revenge)." Is this a pastoral counsel to love the enemy? Not quite. We are to "learn to believe for certain that whatever our enemy has *wickedly* committed against us was permitted and sent by God's *just* dispensation."[24] In other words, wickedness is just. Of course, few Calvinists (beyond Jerry Falwell) used this logic to legitimate the attack on the Twin Towers.

Yet the logic-defying logic of omnipotence twinned with goodness ultimately sanctions *every* injustice as the will of God. This is a Christianity distant from the prophetic traditions of the three Abrahamisms, in which God opposes injustice. In these prophetic traditions, it is up to the faithful neither to justify the injustice as God's will nor to seek revenge, but to *enact* God's justice. Historically, of course, there remains plenty of room for ambiguity—both in biblical models, as in the annihilation of the citizens of Jericho, and in present circumstances, when preemptive violence must perhaps sometimes be risked. Ideally we prevent the build-up of vengefulness that irrupts in a Munich or a Manhattan. Less ideally, a preemptive strike can be justified before the world in the case of imminent rather than fabricated threat. But the Bush doctrine of preemption has sought legitimacy not in terms of defense (mere reaction) but as the promotion of America's "interest in a benevolent international order." America's secular theologians of empire portray it as, like God, omnipresent in its benevolence. Kaplan and Kristol say, "American preeminence cannot be maintained from a distance. The US should instead conceive of itself as at once a European power, an Asian power and of course, a Middle Eastern power. It would act as if threats to the interests of our allies are threats to us, which indeed they are."[25] So it is not just that it will project power unilaterally anywhere it wants. It will also, like God, be already everywhere. As with Calvin, so with the United States. This omnipresence means not just involvement, but control.

The American myth of providential exceptionalism, however, remains complex. From our national foundations it inscribes not only imperial but both revolutionary and democratizing codes. And arguably it was deeply wounded by the 9/11 attack. So I have not argued that the doctrine of omnipotence "caused" the doctrine of preemption. Legitimation is not about causal explanation. Rather, the relation resembles what complexity theory calls a "resonance," in which positive feedback rapidly amplifies a coded pattern. This feedback loop—or halo—has been developing for millennia. But its current American code is unprecedented, not only in its sense of sanctity but also in its apocalyptic weaponry and its global reach. Therefore, *theological* complacency—however much supplemented by progressive activism—will leave untouched the legitimacy of its project.

Despite my deployment of Calvin as an example of a deleterious concept of power, I hasten to add that Calvin is no less important for the delegitimation of the U.S. domination project. In Calvin's theology, any construction of any group—any nation, any race, any religion—as unambiguously good, sin-free agents of divine vengeance counts only as crassest idolatry. How then could Reformed Protestantism play such a key role in the development of U.S. culture not only in the creative and progressive evolution of its communal disciplines, but also in the spirit of capitalism as well as the worship of human power? A discerning theopolitics reads its guiding texts with constructive ambivalence.

Niebuhr, for instance, took the bull of his own Calvinism by the horns. He embraced the Calvinism that affirms "the grace of divine power, working without immediate regard for the virtues or defects of its recipients (as illustrated by the sun shining 'upon the evil and the good and the rain descending upon the just and the unjust')."[26] But he shows how "any grateful acceptance of God's uncovenanted mercies is easily corrupted from gratitude to self-congratulation" when it "represents particular divine acts directly correlated to particular human and historical situations"—when, in other words, it yields to the logic of omnipotence. Niebuhr shows the roots of the American Protestant identification of *affluence* with *blessing* in Calvin himself, who declared that "there is no question that riches should be in the portion of the godly rather than the wicked, for godliness hath the promise in this life as well as the life to come."[27] In the formative period of the union, American prosperity seems to have widely supported the notion of our special favor: "If any people have been lifted up to advantages and privileges, we are the people." Thus wrote William Stoughton (1631–1703). "We have had the eye and hand of God working everywhere for our good."[28] But it is precisely here that our acute sense of sin is sabotaged by our notion of preemptive providence, which fosters our world-threatening innocence.

One paragraph in Niebuhr's chapter entitled "The American Future" made my hair stand on end. Writing over a half-century ago, he warned that our technocratic notion that history can be mastered like nature

> could tempt us to lose patience with the tortuous course of history. We might be driven to hysteria by its inevitable frustrations. We might be tempted to bring the whole of modern history to a tragic conclusion by one final and mighty effort to overcome its frustrations. The political term for such an effort is "preventive war." It is

not an immediate temptation; but it could become so in the next decade or two. A democracy can not, of course, engage in an explicit preventive war.[29]

But we *have*: explicitly, doctrinally, and without imminent or even eventual threat to ourselves. And in its aftermath, the democratic experiment hangs in the balance.

After Omnipotence

A theology of omnipotence electrifies the halo of American domination. Where then does the idolatry lie—in the fact that the United States plays God or, as I would put it, in the fact that it imitates a *false* God? Does the idolatry lie in our emulation of a divine superpower or in our confusion of God with omnipotence in the first place? A theopolitics of omnipotence is clearly at work in imperialism. But is there imperialism within the doctrine of omnipotence?

Whitehead, neither an idealist nor a realist but both, it was again who wrote, concerning the conversion of the Roman Empire to Christianity, of "the deeper idolatry, of the fashioning of God in the image of the Egyptian, Persian, and Roman imperial rulers." Pointing out one effect of this idolatry, he said that the resulting doctrine of "a transcendent creator, at whose fiat the world came into being, and whose imposed will it obeys, is the fallacy which has infused tragedy into the histories of Christianity and of [Islam]." Then comes one of the great propositions of Christian auto-critique: "The church gave unto God the attributes that belonged exclusively to Caesar."[30]

There you have pretty much the origin of what is called process theology, whose leading exponents still fan the flames of that flickering Galilean humility. Its God, who works by "lure" rather than domination, cannot therefore legitimate projects of dominance. David Griffin has called this a shift from the power of coercion to the power of persuasion—the democratic art par excellence.[31]

But impotence is not the only alternative to Calvinistic omnipotence. Another alternative discerns at the heart of the universe a wisdom of open ends, a strange attractor amid indeterminacy and its complex determinations. Calvin is right: God is not sitting in a watchtower, impassively awaiting the blowback. God is there, in the midst of every event. But Calvin assumed that to *participate* in an event is to *control* it. Yes, God remembers every sparrow, numbers every hair. But does this mean—as Calvin in defending double predestination says—that God *determines* which of my hairs will turn grey today? I do affirm with Calvin that "God" names a dark incomprehensibility, not to be reduced to the anthropomorphic terms of human love or justice—thus Job's bewildering whirlwind. But then why reduce the mystery to an all-too-human, all-too-masculine, and all-too-imperial idol of *power*? Why turn a humbling mystery into a mystification of injustice?

Many Christians are ready for an alternative to an assumption of God's omnipotence, for a transcoding of cosmic power. It also has resonance for many Jews, Muslims, Hindus, Buddhists, seekers, and agnostics of various sorts. For there is an ocean of *satyagraha*, of truth-force, waiting to surge into this new millennium. Faith everywhere is on the verge of coming of age. It is in part blocked by incredulity—even many thoughtful people assume that faith requires some big guy in the sky. They are repelled by the theopolitics of power. They can see on the one hand *a manic will to power called omnipotence* and on the other a *depressive sentimentality called love*. For the classical fusion of goodness with omnipotence creates in fact not unity but a profoundly conflicted entity.

To heal the internally contradictory religious combination of love and power, power itself first needs recoding. Then another kind of love, a divinely *infinite desire*, might make itself felt—a desire that is the opposite, as the Jewish philosopher Emmanuel Levinas suggests, of an *imperial totality*. Such a love desires our fullest becoming—our *genesis*—as individuals, as peoples, as religions, as nations, as creatures inextricably embedded within the interdependencies of the creation. It therefore lets responsibility for the well-being of the earth fall squarely back on the shoulders of us earthlings. As the matrix of spiritual codes is enriched by process, liberation, feminist, and ecological theologians,[32] these theologians support a range of movements that Richard Falk identifies with "globalization from below."[33] They do not reject the politics of theology or the theology of politics, but move desirously toward a theopolitics of becoming.

The Spirit of this wider, wilder, achingly beautiful creation does sometimes seem to be revealing itself, but not making itself known—we only *know* our own metaphors. So we might make them as rich in justice and "care that nothing be lost," as poetically alive and even scripturally resonant as possible. Let the hierarchical universe of uni-lateral and omnipotent sovereignty fade into a more wildly democratic cosmos of unpredictable and uncontrollable—but never unordered—interrelations. God is called upon not as a unilateral superpower but as a relational force, not an omnipotent creator from nothing, imposing order upon chaos, but the lure to a self-organizing complexity, creat-ing out of the chaos—the *tohuvabohu* of which Genesis 1 speaks. Recall that for Arendt legitimacy entails narratives of creation, indeed, birth narratives. How would such a shift—to a narrative of beginnings that is more faithful both biblically and materially—alter the creation's codes of legitimation? Might the world begin to appear not as the work of a preemptive transcendence, nor of random chance, but of the unpredictable, uncontrollable, and uncontrolling wisdom of the whirlwind?

This theology does not apologize for uncertainty. Faith is not about certainty but about courage.[34] Faith takes the primordial American value of liberty to heart: nothing important can be imposed by coer-cion. Freedom will not be achieved by dominance, legitimacy by lies, law by unilateralism, peace by war, Christian love by hatred of the Other. That coercive, imperialistic spirituality needs to be replaced by a democratizing spirituality.

The American democratic ideal has always been limited by its imprint of empire, class, race, gender, sex, and even species injustice. So has Christian love. Might we augment both? Can we broadcast to our people this self-evident truth—that human democracy, like love, will not legitimate any project of global dominance? Democracy either extends to our international relations or dies at home—before we ever quite give it birth.

PART TWO

OF BEASTS AND WHORES

Examining
Our
Political
Unconscious

3

Territory, Terror, and Torture: Dreamreading the Apocalypse

My personal apocalypse radar recently led me to a mesmerizing work of what is called cyberpunk literature, *Hard-Boiled Wonderland and the End of the World*.[1] Haruki Murakami's protagonist starts off in a high-tech labyrinth beneath the surface of postmodern Tokyo; he ends up, after a variety of off-beat apocalyptic adventures, in a space described as Zeno's paradox, a state of virtual immortality, that is, of the infinite subdivision of time. Here he will be locked eternally outside of the world and inside of his unconscious. Within a strangely static space, resembling an underpopulated medieval village, where people have been violently separated from their shadows, he has been designated "the Dreamreader." With his fingers he reads the skulls of unicorns for their old dreams.

The Whore and the Messiah

Within the virtual space of the present time, might *dreamreading* be an apt trope for biblical hermeneutics? What if we read the Christian apocalypse as an old dream—and the Bible as a dream library? Given its antiquity, the dream of apocalypse, specifically, has a peculiar vitality.[2] As visionary text and as cultural habit, it reverberates through every rhetoric of the End of the World, every scenario of final battle and holy war, of "we are good and they are evil." Armageddon-style antagonism is not confined to Christian, Jewish, or Muslim war-makers, however. The utopianism of the left is equally rooted in the biblical apocalyptic tradition. So when progressive hopes for history are disappointed, the righteous despair (*de/spes*: "loss of hope") that we are sliding toward the endtime apocalypse. Besides, who can follow world news without occasional attacks of end-of-the-world panic?

In the hard-boiled wonderland of the post-9/11 United States, engagement of the Apocalypse itself—as text and habit—may help all of us to face our apocalyptic shadows. In an interview soon after the attack, Edward Said noted that "it was not meant to be argued with. . . . It transcended the political and moved into the metaphysical." He was countering the immediate discursive fusion—under the sign of "terror"—of territorial struggles (like the Palestinians') with the Al Qaeda megaterrorism. "There was a kind of cosmic, demonic quality of mind at work here, which refused to have any interest in dialogue and political organization and persuasion."[3] Simultaneously, the international lawyer Richard Falk called bin Laden's violence "apocalyptic terrorism."[4] Both of these thoroughly secular thinkers, with no interest in demonizing resistance to U.S. imperialism, nonetheless reached spontaneously into the vocabulary of apocalypse to capture this sense of the nonnegotiable absolute. In *Terror in the Mind of God* Mark Juergensmeyer argued that "religious concepts of cosmic war . . . are ultimately beyond historical control, even though they are identified with this-worldly struggle. A satanic enemy cannot be transformed: it can only be destroyed."[5] Taking a hermeneutical leap backwards, a dreamreader might note that indeed the Apocalypse of John displays no interest in transforming the Roman Empire or even individual sinners: "For the time is near. Let the evildoer still do evil, the filthy still be filthy, and the righteous still do right" (Rev. 22:11). There is a compelling organizational force to this nonnegotiable dichotomy of good and evil, a sense of settled moral clarity amid the terrors of a time. Were Falk and Said reinscribing the dualism? Or simply describing its new self-revelation?

If the violent American response to the megaterrorism appeared at first more pragmatic and defensive than apocalyptic and visionary, the state soon uncovered its unprecedented new national security strategy. Its doctrine of the preemptive strike, speedily deployed in

Iraq, was the key to world power: "America has, and intends to keep, military strengths beyond challenge, thereby making the destabilizing arms races of other eras pointless, and limiting rivalries to trade and pursuits of peace."[6] This is a straightforward announcement of the Pax Americana, and by an implication widely noted, to building an empire.[7] As in the Roman precedent, the aim of war is peace. "There is nothing bigger than to achieve world peace," Bush had said of his grand goal.[8] "The vision thing," Bush Senior's bane, was Junior's boon. His team envisioned "a global US military empire and a degree of imperial ambition with little, if any, historical parallels."[9] Unlike any European or Asian antecedent, however, this empire donned the face of the apocalyptic messiah. "We are in a conflict between good and evil, and America will call evil by its name." Preempting argument, Bush reassured us that "by confronting evil and lawless regimes, we do not create a problem, we reveal a problem. And we will lead the world in solving it."[10]

What we must recognize as *messianic imperialism* accelerated into full gallop with George W. Bush. Under the globalized conditions of the early millennium, it will continue to tempt even those U.S. policymakers who are sobered by its failures and conscious of its corruptions. The status of sole superpower renders the dream of absolute power well nigh irresistible. So this is my plea: when the imperial reaction reveals, indeed revels in, its apocalyptic messianism, then we as citizen theologians must not only denounce its idolatry but disclose its self-contradiction. For the apocalypse and its Messiah are inherently *anti*-imperialist. Thus all western revolutions, the American and French as well as the Russian, as Ernst Bloch in *The Principle of Hope* demonstrated, are heirs of biblical prophecy and apocalypse.[11] Indeed, the empire in the Book of Revelation is the evil Other, the true enemy, of the apocalyptic Messiah, and is symbolized as the Beast and his whore-queen, Babylon, the imperial city.

So it is a strange hybrid that has appeared upon the horizon of the third millennium. Behold: the Messiah-Whore! The righteous Messiah, the divine warrior with the double-edged sword as a tongue, has merged with its opposite. It isn't the first time. There is a tradition of Christian empire. How else could so many Americans have accepted a born-again Christian whose "favorite philosopher" is Jesus—and who morphed into a Roman-style emperor? Might we read this hybrid messiah/beast as a living dream, as a dramatic persona synthesized of biblical effects, enacted in, but not reducible to, a particular politician, patriarchy, or policy?

The Shadow

If such dreams are alive but largely unconscious, producing new modes of religious violence under the (rather threadbare) cover of a U.S. secular separation of state from religion, it behooves us as religious thinkers to bring the nightmares to light—to make their galloping contradictions conscious. It is not a matter of purging our shadows, of repressing and denying our violent power drives as a people but, to the contrary, of reconnecting us to our shadows. Then there is some chance of taking responsibility rather than persisting in messianic innocence. Shadows, according to the analytical psychologist C. G. Jung, represent repressed parts of ourselves. They are not inherently evil—but may become so if left unclaimed. They form the threshold to a "collective unconscious." I am suggesting that we are dealing here with an *apocalyptic unconscious*. This unconscious is not a space filled with eternal, changeless archetypes. It is rather a subliminal space where our culturally unacceptable shadows—of race, sexuality, greed, power, perhaps even religion—languish. But in its suspended animation it occupies, and at the same time constitutes, a certain political space: that of a paradoxical postmodern territoriality, which is not a literal land with negotiable boundaries but a space akin to terror that can only be maintained by extreme violence. This violence at the edges of our collective consciousness is where any cruelty can be justified by the threat of "Barbarians," "terrorists," "infidels," or "unbelievers"—and is hidden from history.

In this shady space, public power operates with something very like the secrecy of torture—that is, as we shall see with the help of Elaine Scarry's *The Body in Pain*, with a drama of a unilateral power inflicting its illusion of total control on its victims. The implications of this dreamreading for the classical doctrine of omnipotence as well as the neoclassical doctrine of preemption will become apparent: *apocalypto*!

The author of the Christian Apocalypse was himself a timely reader of old dreams, Jewish apocalypses, and the long struggle of Israel with the empires: dreams of messianic liberation in his own century had fomented dangerous acts of opposition to the Babylonian-Roman Beasts of global empire. Resistance to the Roman Empire and its client monarchy, the Herods, had been met with horrific imperial punishment, as in the crucifixion of two thousand protestors outside Jerusalem near the time of Jesus' infancy. The latter's own torture and crucifixion was a narrative microcosm of the colonial violence; onto a single body in pain was mapped all human vulnerability. The death of that particular Jewish Messiah-figure comprised at the time one more loop in the "spiral of violence" leading to the final destruction of the Temple.[12] Worlds were ending, yet the messianic faith could not be exterminated. Nevertheless, it was getting hard-boiled.

Within a dreamscape of apocalypse, the bright Messiah on the white horse—he is, after all, the most developed holy warrior mythologem in the Bible—goes forth in righteousness. Yet he is mirrored by the dark Beast of empire. In John's bitter parody, the Beast, called elsewhere Antichrist, parodies the Christ: he mocks and mimics the Messiah, aping his power, promising peace, sending false prophets. The mirroring is visual: both the Messiah as Lamb of God and the beast as Serpent or devil sport an excess of horns and eyes. It is also sexual: while the Messiah will couple with the heavenly city, the virgin New Jerusalem, the Beast couples with the haughty urban Babylon (Rome). But who, a dreamreader must ask, is mimicking whom? Does the mimesis go only one way? For both cities, the New Jerusalem as well as Rome, war is to bring peace, violence to bring justice, dominance to bring freedom. How should a vulnerable and victimized community fight an empire that bullies and seduces the whole world—except by a secret empire, with armed angelic hosts led by the shining warrior on a white horse, empowered by the transcendent throne of All-Power? John's virtual *basileia*, his "empire of God," shadowboxes with the Roman Empire; leading an army outperforming in militancy any imperial troops, his holy warrior will be as ruthless as any Caesar.

According to postcolonial theorist Homi K. Bhabha, mimicry between oppressor and oppressed ("colonial mimicry") articulates a strange kind of desire, a conflicted envy, indeed a constitutive *ambiva-lence*. The colonized mirrors the colonizer by a kind of warped desire, for the imperial ideal has been not only imposed but internalized. "Empire is the site of immense ambivalence in this book," New Testament scholar Stephen Moore avers, deploying Bhabhan postcolonial theory. "Revelation's overt resistance to and expressed repulsion toward Roman imperial ideology is surreptitiously compromised and undercut by covert compliance and attraction. Not for nothing is Rome figured . . . as a prostitute. . . . What better embodiment, for the seer, of seductive repulsiveness, repulsive seduction?" Thus in Moore's anti-apocalypse "the difficulty of effectively exiting empire by attempting to turn imperial ideology against itself is regularly underrated by those who acclaim Revelation for decisively breaking the relentless cycle of empire."[13] He thus challenges a certain uncritical liberation-theological avowal of apocalypse. I would agree that the apocalyptic mirage of omnipotence doubles and mimics the imperial power that it subversively mocks. In the Book of Revelation the mimicry does not yet constitute a merger and thus a straight self-contradiction. But that anti-imperial mimicry seems to have prepared the way (Lord of Lords and irony of ironies), for the mutation of the early Christian Jewish victims of empire into sixteen centuries of Christian empire-builders. If Christian theology is to counter its own colonial patrilineage, it must work with a methodological ambivalence, the theopolitical content of which comprises what I have called a *counter-apocalypse*.

The historical con/fusion between messianism and imperialism was definitively manifest in the western form of pilgrimage known as the crusade. That tradition has lured the Bush dynasty irresistibly eastward. As a parable of theopolitical hermeneutics, let us read how the capture of Jerusalem during the first crusade was narrated as an enactment of the text of Apocalypse. The eleventh-century eyewitness account of Raymund of Aguiles describes the massacre of the forty thousand Muslim inhabitants, men, women, children as the "just and splendid judgment of God" (see chapter 2). In tight apocalyptic intertextuality, judgment day immediately precedes the new creation. So the day after their massacre, the leaders, weeping with happiness, processed into the Holy Sepulcher; now Raymond writes: "A new day, new joy, new and perpetual gladness, the consummation of our labor and devotion, drew forth from all new words and new songs. . . . This day, I say, marks the justification of all Christianity, the humiliation of paganism, the renewal of our faith."[14] So the graphic literalism of the defeat of Jerusalem could be mapped onto the letter of John's New Jerusalem.

The Apocalypse had Christianized the much older dream of holy war. But it took centuries for Christian powers to begin to enact the symbol in history. The dream smoldered among the Abrahamisms, igniting again in our time as a Caesar-Messiah complex. If the messianic imperialism, provoked again, eerily, by the Muslim "unbelievers," yields this doubled, self-divided construct, this Messiah-Beast—might its peculiar hybridity afford at least a certain internal dividedness and so a resistance to what Jacques Derrida called ominously "the totalitarianization of democracy"? But what sort of space, what sort of territory, does a counter-apocalypse reveal, disclose, open up?

It was as apocalyptic vision that a local, territorializing Israelite faith became ever more global. It formed first as a response to the imperial aggression of Babylon, which had traumatically deterritorialized Israel; then the Babylon of the Isaianic apocalypse became John's code for Rome. The homeland was centered in Jerusalem, charged with the messianic nationalism of liberation, and morphed into the transcendent Christian (non)space. Later, the *utopia*—literally "no place"—deterritorialized Jerusalem, the trope of the New Jerusalem, but it was recurrently reterritorialized. Of this the Crusaders' conflation of Jerusalem with the New Jerusalem provides one example and the recent reterritorialization of evil Babylon as Saddam's Baghdad another. The concept of a complementary oscillation between "deterritorialization" and "reterritorialization" has enabled the philosophers Gilles Deleuze and Felix Guattari to rethink the flows of power and resistance in human history.

That reterritorializing messianic spiral shoots in and out of discursive visibility. It seems in late modernity to disappear behind the coolly secular determinism of economic globalization—a totalizing deterritorialization—driven by motives of competition and profit indifferent to religion (and increasingly, to *nation*). But had a financialization of the globe not already been prefigured as the demonic force, the imperial Other, of John's Apocalypse? In the Apocalypse, the Great Whore is depicted as fornicating especially with three groups: the client kings of the empire, the merchants, and the mercantile sea captains, by whom trade became global. The culminating chapters of Revelation depict their despair at the loss of all that global wealth: "The merchants of these wares, who gained wealth from her, will stand far off, in fear of her torment, weeping and mourning aloud, 'Alas, alas, the great city, clothed in fine linen, in purple and scarlet, adorned with gold, with jewels, and with pearls!' For in one hour all this wealth has been laid waste!"(18:15-17). It doesn't take a premillennial, pre-tribulation fundamentalist to think of the single hour it took for the World Trade Towers to collapse.[15]

Vis-à-vis Christian imperialisms and their politico-economic consequences, Derrida coined another telling term, "globalatinization."[16] While considering the Roman and Roman Catholic doubling of power—with its later English translations—as a "hyper-imperialist appropriation" circulated always in religious language, he did not note the apocalyptic paradox at its base. The prototypical *enemy* of the apocalypse—the Latin Beast or Whore of Empire—has become the primary symbol of the cultural Christianity that has surrounded the globe with its slick aura of sex, stuff, and violence.

Terror and Territory

The protagonist of *Hard-Boiled Wonderland* was stranded in the End of the World forever through a secret brain code, secret even to the protagonist inside whose brain the transaction occurred. The program for the code was called "end of the world." This Tokyo scientist ended up in Finland. But the hard-boiled wonderland is anywhere and nowhere. It is the very dream of information-globalization.[17] Both the deterritorializing forces of high-tech-info-economic globalization and the reterritorializing passions of the Abrahamic traditions seem to act out—as in a dream—an apocalyptic unconscious. And in a uniquely formative way, the "end of the world" belongs—as omega to alpha—to the U.S. code of origin, of our own "new creation" as the "new world," *novus ordo seclorum*. . . .

Might we let the Messiah-Beast binary symbolize the tension between territorialization and deterritorialization? This tension has always energized the mobile Abrahamic faiths, and nowhere more clearly than in their apocalyptic moments, when the yearning for a sacred space, for the purity and security of a *territory*, is invested with *terror*.[18] The aggressive *particularism* of these claims consists precisely in their *universalism*: the bounded identity carries a boundless demand.

Analogously the postmodern secularization of this tension takes place between a *trans*national empire of economics, as it pulls down "barriers to free trade," and a religio-nationalist *terra firma*, the securely bounded and unified "homeland"—between the secular have-a-nice-day desires Disneyfying, Coca-colating, IBMing, and General Motoring the globe and the dream of a securely bounded existence in a homeland, a Jerusalem, of one's own.[19] The first *deterritorializes* its subjects; the other *reterritorializes* them. The two operations together seem to comprise a formidable dialectic of terrestrial domination.

Our particular nationalism has always needed bolstering by the Judeo-Christian civil religion—"God Bless America"—in order to create the feeling of homeland, of *we*. "We" can never easily reterritorialize our U.S. identity. Our nationality, so tenuously, so superficially rooted in its own land, is in fact based on migratory, indeed genocidal, and increasingly ecocidal uprootings. It has no longer (if it ever did have) any chance of racial or ethnic unification that would not comprise the most violent division. Indeed for this reason our territorial nationalism may actually depend upon appeal to the imperial messianism (as the tawdry code of reterritorialization, "God Bless America" and "United We Stand," seems to indicate). The *otro mundo* ("other" world) as the new creation for Columbus, the City on the Hill for the Puritans, Manifest Destiny as we moved to invade the Spanish territories—all signal our distinctively apocalyptic justification of conquest.

"Narcissism is the other face of Judgment." Touching the nerve of this dream-laden sense of territory, Edward Ingebretsen analyzes the peculiar territoriality of the American apocalypse. He finds in Manifest Destiny the narcissistic universalization of an American eschatology, or vision of the endtimes. "Manifest Destiny could be read onto new-world geographies partly because its terms had already been established as a moral geography by which to map the wild terrain of the soul." Apocalypse thus provides a map for every detail of life, in its intimate interiority and its most aggressive territorial expansion. The formative U.S. homiletics of Final Judgment may have invested territoriality forever with terror. Our founding myth pulls us backwards toward end things: "*Nostalgia and its twin, terror.*"[20]

Yet these old territorial dreams remain in tension with the secular pieties of financial globalization, with its *de*territorializing effects. At the same time, biblical anti-imperialism also reverberates in the American founding mythology, reinscribing the original biblical fusion of exodus with new creation codes. A forceful undercurrent of liberation as conquest fuels U.S. rhetoric of "freedom"—a militant messianism not of empire but of exodus into the (inconveniently inhabited but) "Promised Land."

We need not interpret the doctrine of preemption, the militarized Pax Americana, and U.S.-based global capitalism as blended smoothly in some totalizing process of uniform imperial unfolding. If the dominant dialectic is at odds with itself, if the Messiah-Whore figure symbolically encodes profound tensions, they may also suggest openings for creative resistance. According to Falk, a self-contradictory synthesis is indeed being attempted between the territorial force of patriotic nationalism and the nonterritorial thrust of the economic globalization, which it serves.[21] The flag-waving cascade of nationalist kitsch unleashed by the collapse of the Trade Towers at first signaled the shock of atrocity, of an unprecedented vulnerability upon our own territory (and thus of the impossibility of "owning" *terra* at all). But "our emotions were being hijacked by the government," writes ethicist Ada María Isasi-Díaz, "in an attempt . . . to keep us from thinking about how part of the responsibility for what happened lies squarely on the shoulders of this nation."[22] This sense of responsibility does not justify terrorism as a strategy of resistance. It does require our understanding that in the face of the crushing deterritorialization of other nations by an Americanized consumer culture, not to mention its reterritorialization by our military, terror may seem to be the only way to defend one's *terra*. But destructive modes of resistance, operating out of their own deformed messianism of reterritorialization, only empower the dialectic of domination.

Domination feeds on terror. Thus Lee Quinby has written of a "gothic fearscape" produced by U.S. discourses and practices of security. "This generates, in turn, gothic subjects who seek omnipotent protection and submit themselves to surveillance and control at the expense of their freedom."[23] This fantasy of omnipotence roots in the least democratic of messianic impulses, in the childlike passivity of subjects yearning for a security that can never exist beyond infancy but whose semblance can be erected at the cost of our freedom. Ingebretsen's discernment of the oscillation of an infantile narcissism and a final judgment suggests, similarly, the projection of an early American gothic upon the current globe.

Our messianic territorialism can temporarily nationalize the sacred. It can sacralize narcissistic yearnings for closure. But in this the territorializing closure bumps up against the economic theory of "openness." This doctrine of openness serves the ends of global corporations, for whom nationality is increasingly a matter of convenience and "freedom" a semantic container for oil, cheap labor, and other "interests." Thus this oscillation between territorialization and deterritorialization appears in the provocative *Empire*, by Michael Hardt and Antonio Negri, strongly influenced by Deleuze and Guattari. Their book focuses on the *deterritorializing* push of the new Empire. Indeed, written before 9/11, it strongly resists identifying the postmodern empire with the United States or with any nation state, for the new style of "sovereignty" fluidly displaces the rigid boundaries of the modern nation.[24] Postmodern narcissism tries to shake off its gothic shadows, trading nostalgia for a neon greed.

In letting the Messiah-Lamb/Whore-Beast dramatize the tension of territorialization and deterritorialization, I have noted both a secular form of the tension, that between nationalism and globalization, and a religious form, that between religious nationalism and its global, universalizing drive. In its current manifestation, the mimicry of messianic Lamb by imperial Beast—or is it vice versa?—generates a formidable *geopolitical* force field. But we are trying to map this imperial expansion onto a *theopolitical* territoriality. In this space the tension between the boundary-busting universality of empire and the boundary-hardening patriotism of nation takes on an apocalyptic poignancy. The strange yearning for home is displaced from the origins of the nation itself to its messianic aspirations. Between nostalgia and terror, home is always still . . . *coming.* This eschatological postponement of a blessing we feel we have coming to us—this can be torture.

The Book of Torture

The mimicry within the text takes a painfully embodied form. As the Lamb is said to show the marks of slaughter, one of the heads of the Beast "seemed to have received a death-blow, but the plague of its death had been healed." It performs a triple parody: it mimics the mortal wound, the death by torture, and the resurrection of the Lamb. So "in amazement the whole earth followed the beast." Following this doubling of the wound, we may find ourselves, if not amazed, knee-deep in the torturous maze of religious violence. Indeed the Book of Revelation is full of tortured bodies. The damned suffer eternal agony in the lake of fire, along with the beasts (20:15; 21:8). And it is through torture that the misogyny of the text gets satisfaction: when the Great Whore falls, it is not enough to announce her destruction; she is subjected to a ritual of sexual torture, stripped naked, raped, cooked, and eaten. Moreover, the woman who shines like the sun, the so-called Queen of Heaven, is said to suffer birth pangs like torture—the word used, *basinizomai*, for her speechless cries (12:2) is not otherwise used of birth but signifies testimony given by slaves under torture.

Of torture, Elaine Scarry has written that it reduces the other to a mere body without speech. Torture is built "upon repeated acts of display." Because it has "as its purpose the production of a fantastic illusion of power, torture is a grotesque piece of compensatory drama."[25] For it is "precisely because the reality of that power is so highly contestable, the regime is so unstable, that torture is being used." Or one might rather say that the power is unstable but nonetheless real: it is the dream of its invulnerable omnipotence that comprises the illusion. One might read the Jewish and Christian victims of Roman torture, the martyrs, as dramatizing in their bodily pain both the superpower status of Rome and in their anti-imperial witness, encoded by John, its absolute instability.

In the Apocalypse, however, *God's* enemies also get tortured. So what instability of agency is John compensating for, or repressing, in the ritual torture of the enemies of the Messiah? Could it be the omnipotence of God that is so highly contestable? Is the regime of invisible divine power not terribly difficult to believe in, especially when history seems—as it so often does—to be going the other way? What is more theologically unstable than the dream of divine control? Does the Book of Revelation, like torture, thus achieve what Scarry calls "the conversion of real pain into the fiction of power"? She does not mention the apocalypse. But she comes close: "intense pain," she writes, "is world-destroying."[26]

Yet the world-destruction of the great fictional battles of the book are narrated as wars against a collective enemy, not just as torture of symbolic individuals. The ancient myth of the divine warrior finds here its fullest biblical form. The Babylonian Marduk who slays the goddess Tiamat has morphed into the holy warrior who brings down

obvious analogue to torture is war," writes Scarry. "War and torture
have the same two targets, a people and its civilization." But while
war is a "reciprocal activity of injuring to produce a nonreciprocal
outcome," torture is a symbolic ritual of nonreciprocal power, enacted
on the small scale. But when it comes to weapons of mass destruction,
war "in all its new massiveness" actually conforms "to the model of
torture rather than that of conventional war."[27] Ultimately the battles
of John's Apocalypse are fought by supernatural superpowers and
destroy whole populations. The clash of the armies at Armageddon
is a pretense of reciprocal vulnerability. So biblical genocide also conforms to the structure of torture. The Book of Revelation can be read
as the Book of Torture.

No more can the apocalyptic style of assault now conducted by the
United States (with or without weapons of mass destruction) pretend
to a warlike reciprocity. We enact—with transcendent detachment
from the pain—the drama of fire raining down from above on helpless populations. Our technology has realized an apocalyptic dream
of divine power: "And fire came down from the sky and consumed
them" (20:9). Then immediately the first of the seven angels blows
his trumpet. . . . Apocalypse operates by a supreme preemption, a unilateral infliction of pain, the preview of which strengthens faith in its
ultimate victory. Similarly, the new U.S. preemption, with its massive
proleptic build-up, intends to strengthen faith in "freedom"—if not of
democracy, certainly the infallible system of "open" market competition supported by a new militarization. We will so terrify our potential
enemies by the guarantee of their unilateral destruction, should they
threaten our "interests," that they will submit as impotently as victims
of torture.[28]

Or at least that was the plan. The traditional U.S. taboo against torture itself has been broken: since 9/11 various admissions of the out-
sourced torture of our prisoners have been publicized.[29] Then came
the news of the torture of prisoners in the Iraqi prison Abu Ghraib
by U.S. military personnel. I did not expect the ensuing silence of the
religious right. This, I thought, would shake them out of the dream
of U.S. righteousness. Then I remembered John's Apocalypse. Fortunately, feminists did not remain defensively silent about the role of
women. A "kind of feminist naivete died" when the photos came out,
wrote Barbara Ehrenreich immediately. "If you were doing PR for Al

Qaeda, you couldn't have staged a better picture to galvanize misogy-nist Islamic fundamentalists around the world." [30] An MP in England who had supported the war was heard to fulminate over the BBC: "We have had enough of these Appalachian Jezebels." So the apocalypse hovers by, modeling the displacement of blame for systemic violation onto the sexual sadism of a female. But only a feminism that under-stands women as innocent victims of masculine power or as naturally disposed to mutuality in the exercise of agency will be stunned by the evil women do. It is the larger question of power, with its divine right to punish and destroy, that must continuously push us in our theopo-litical meditations to the questioning of omnipotence itself.

Omnipotence, Territory, and Torture

The proposed Pax Americana projects a godlike power, a providential omnipotence so threatening that resistance and war are to be ren-dered obsolete. Its nationalist territorialism has from the outset been yoked to the corollary, deterritorializing project of the *pax economica*. *The National Security Strategy* of September 2002 defines this peace by militarization as a tool of economic openness. The *Strategy* virtuously vows "to extend the peace by encouraging free and open societies on every continent" to "expand the circle of development by open-ing societies"[31]—whether or not they want to be "opened."[32] Indeed the dogma of openness has been the key, argues Andrew Bacevich in *American Empire*, to U.S. geopolitics for a century—the need for more and more markets in which to sell our goods, without which we can neither "grow" nor maintain, he notes, our own unacknowledged class structure at home.[33]

This openness echoes perversely in Scarry's analysis of violence: torture and war "open the bodies" of the Other. If the body is terri-tory, torture reduces it to nothing but body, mere uncultured matter. Torture deterritorializes the body, as empire deterritorializes the land. This opening of the body violates boundaries, as does the post-modern economic order. "This dissolution of the boundary between inside and outside gives rise to . . . an almost obscene conflation of private and public."[34] Hence the humiliation of the one-sided power thrusts. This opening through violence mirrors not accidentally the structure of sexual violence.[35] And during this same period, as Richard Goldstein puts it, "the once-mocked figure of the dominant male has become a real-life hero. Saluting the new spirit of patriarchal vitality, *People* included [U.S. Secretary of Defense Donald] Rumsfeld in its most recent list of the sexiest men alive. In his feckless swagger we see the timeless union of militarism and macho."[36] Or as Lee Quinby phrases it, we witness a renewal of the trinity of "militarism, messianism and masculinism."[37] If, in the political philosophy of the period, the embrace of war was a transcendence of the Vietnam syndrome, was it not by the same token—and as evidenced in the encroachment of anti-abortion policies—a transcendence of feminism?

Yet the Apocalypse itself runs counter to the idolatry of invulnerable hypermasculinity. Both the Lamb and the Beast display their gynomorphic openings, their wounds. They expose an inevitable mutuality of wounding. In their mimicry they nearly sabotage the dream of superpower, the dream of impassionability. Almost they cry for compassion. "There will be no more tears." *Apocalypto*: to reveal, to disclose, to open—it opens up its bodies, even the divine body—in the hope of a world without violence. It displays the unmaking of the world—and its remaking. But its remaking takes place through unmaking, its redemption through destruction. "Your wrath has come and the time . . . for destroying those who destroy the earth" (11:18). That final discreation (one that offers some comfort to environmentalism) serves as the prelude to new creation. And we do not want to miss the truth of the destruction that is inseparable from any creation. The ill lies elsewhere.

Unlike prior prophetic eschatologies of the new creation trauma, the early Christian apocalyptic hope developed an allergy to human finitude itself. "For there will be no more death." It is not just a matter of ending unjust death and the tears of victims—but of terminating all mourning, all indeterminacy, all vulnerability. This new hope dreams the dream of absolute omnipotence. Perhaps more than in any other canonized text, events of consequence can be read off a predetermined future. If the Beast is able to slaughter, it is because he has been "given authority" to make martyrs, so unjust death is encrypted as redemptive sacrifice. Yet the text still oscillates between a phantasm of total power and knowledge and the much older imago of the *Chaoskampf* (the creation of the world by the primal defeat of chaos). The divine warrior is not omnipotent—just powerful. He must still destroy the enemies, the waters and monsters of chaos. Omnipotence by contrast creates *ex nihilo*: it has always already defeated the chaos. It wants "no more sea"—no more *tehom* (Hebrew for "ocean"; Gen. 1:2), no more ghosts of the oceanic mother Tiamat. It yearns for a perfect order, a *pax apocalyptica*, contained within the walls of its New Jerusalem: hard-boiled wonderland indeed. Its dream cannot abide the primal deep in which—according to a very different biblical tradition—any actual creativity unfolds.[38]

But could its clientele actually tolerate such calm stasis? The whole text is turbulent with violent excitement, with a wild energy of unacknowledged chaos, with a holiness of fire, explosion, torment, and bliss. Hence war journalist Chris Hedge's *War Is a Force That Gives Us Meaning*. Is this why apocalyptic justice requires that the damned be tortured forever, so the intensity of violence can permanently energize the utopia? Violence bursts boundaries between inside and out, self and other; it ruptures the boundaries of any body. And as embodied in the holy monsters of apocalypse, Lamb or Beast, violence transgresses simultaneously the animal and divine boundaries of the human. Like sex, it takes place at the chaotic edge, the eschaton, of our experience. The constructive work of theology surely requires now a more honest embrace of that chaos, that frightening and exciting uncertainty at the edge of our experience—if we actually desire a creative alternative to the nightmarish repression of the chaos in the name of an order and a good that tortures, exploits, or annihilates the dark, chaotic Other as evil itself.

Earth Dreams

The messianic good-versus-evil superheroism of the Pax Americana distinguishes an American from a Roman Empire. Belief in our power as not just superior but good sustains the myth of the reluctant superpower, of a vigorous New World "deluded," as Reinhold Niebuhr saw it, "by the concept of our innocency." But as long as the belief commonly persists, as indeed the common sense of believers, that omnipotence *is* godlike, that one transcendent power *can* destroy evil once and for all, then they will also assume that a virtuous violence will bring about a final peace. The theopolitical problem is not just that a nation pretends to a godlike unilateral power, but that *unilat-*

eral power still appears as godlike at all. The idolatry of a "divine" finite sovereignty is exceeded only by the divinization of sovereignty itself. Historically, divine omnipotence was only achieved as a mimicry of empire. It was intended to mock and compete with the already divinized forms of pagan empire. It did so successfully. But the resultant Christian empires carry the internal contradiction, at once explosively self-deceptive and potentially a valuable source of self-criticism, of the messianic *anti*-imperialism.

Those my seminary professor Alan O. Miller called the "sibling rivals of the family of Abraham" did not invent religious violence. But they have failed to bring about a more peaceful or even sustainable world. Their distinctive genius emanates from a monotheistic concentration of the Spirit at the edge of history: a force not identical with any history and not separate from history itself. They have therefore contributed to the species a theopolitical vision of justice and mercy as possible and therefore as imperative. This gift comes from their shared notion—if I may paraphrase it in terms sisterly to it—that the creative Wisdom of the universe holds her human stewards responsible for the state of their world and its mutually vulnerable bodies. But that monotheistic concentration combined with a certain Platonic idealism to produce the hard-boiled omnipotence above, with its apocalyptic shadow realm below.

A theology that seeks to re-embody Spirit in a world of mutually vulnerable bodies deconstructs the "God of power and might." It questions the entire doctrinal arsenal of omnipotence: divine sovereignty, aseity and impassionability, irresistible grace, *creatio ex nihilo*, the exclusive incarnation and revelation in Christ, Final Judgment. These dogmas spin scriptural metaphors into the metanarrative of transcendent power. They belong to the ancient abstractive process whereby Christianity was first imperialized. And key to the deterritorializing and reterritorializing dynamism of Christian empire was the all-male God and his all-male priesthood. This idol of hypermasculinity rises over the land again. He blows Wisdom out of the waters.

At this point, in the face of the moral atrocity of each of the Abrahamisms, some of us still reread the old dreams. We work to heal the nightmares. The imaginary idea of omnipotence could evolve into a cosmically democratized ideal of co-creativity. New resonances between the religions produce an alternative, but still messianic, intensity, with an attractive vocabulary of spiritual pluralism. This pluralism respects the particular ecologies of every species as the context for any body's agency; it deterritorializes and reterritorializes socio-religious contexts in the interest of a counter-apocalypse that is at the same time a counter-globalization. Rather than the imperial "globalization from above," it participates in a "globalization from below," as Richard Falk describes it—a sustainable catholicity of creaturely solidarity kin to "democratic cosmopolitanism."

A theopolitics of "just love"[39] is rediscovering the *cosmos* of cosmopolitanism. In this space, creation is renewed, not as a new creation out of nothing, but as the renewal of the creation from within its own shadowed potentiality. The bad dreams of a species locked outside of its own world, cut off from its shadows by violence and ideation, will only be healed from within, because the "within" contains the codes of its own self-overcoming. So we tap and finger the skulls. Is the proper epistemology here eschatological, or political, or gothic—the rapture, democracy, or the horrific last things?

4
Ms.Calculating the Endtimes: Gender Styles of Apocalypse

I am the first and the last.
I am the honored one and the scorned one.
I am the whore and the holy one.
     —*Thunder: Perfect Mind*, Nag Hammadi Codex

What does sex have to do with apocalypse—with a mythic war between a sword-tongued Messiah who in the End lives happily ever after with his bejeweled Virgin, and a majestic urban Whore with her beastly paramours? More or less everything, at the level of the dream. But then again, not much, at the level of its intentions—the marks of gender and the revelations of sex in the Book of Revelation are symbolic of more or less everything *but* sex. As the energies of sex and gender surge through the entire network of our most private and most collective lives, so they also pulse through the texts and the traditions of the religious imagination. This chapter attempts to transcode a certain apocalyptic form of the gender binary. It brings a feminist lens to our theopolitical investigations. Or rather, it makes explicit and central the feminist perspective that has from the start motivated a counter-apocalypse.

Pumping for Apocalypse

Apocalyptic movements emanate from a marginal, readily underestimated power, a powder keg of language ever ready to explode into practice. These movements are radical, whether revolutionary or reactionary, and they are often—though pointedly not always—aggressively misogynist. They represent a wide swathe of "subjugated discourses," popular or arcane, in Foucault's sense (though he did not investigate millennialisms). The last will be first, will finally have their chance. The Second Coming signals a second chance for the losers of history, victims of oppression or of dissipation. And in the more bitter and usually sexist variants, true to the original, their enemies (those whores, those fornicating beasts, those sons of *bitches*) will get their comeuppance.

Of course the defiant rage is often defanged. The repetitive replays of endtime expectations, disappointments, and displacements have lent the whole drama an aura of kitsch, like the soft-porn graphics—indispensable to dispensationalist pamphlets—of the whore of Babylon clad scantily in red, astride her many-headed beast. Reflecting on another scene of apocalyptic stereotypes, Jeff MacGregor described "Wrestlemania" as "the end of the world as we know it." Reading the "seemingly inexplicable resurgence of professional wrestling" as the harbinger of doom, he quipped that "the apocalypse will be televised." And he was aware of the hypertrophy of pertinent scholarship: "1990's red-hot growth sector for media analysis: apocalypse theory."[1] He neglected, however, to comment on the gender regression embodied in these bizarre heroes of postmodern hulkdom. Perhaps it seemed obvious. But sometimes signs of the times are so obvious, so in our face, that we miss their meaning. Costumed in comic book melodrama, the most cartoonish exaggeration of bang-pow masculinity was "coming again." MacGregor couldn't have known how *prophetic* his bit of pop culture analysis would prove. On the other side of the millennium divide, we have seen a second body-builder elected as the governor of a state. Surrounded with the oscillating messianic/demonic images of the nuclear Armageddon movies, the "Terminator" came to office also dubbed "the Grope." He combined apocalyptic and sexist fantasy with Hollywood hyperproduction. Thus is the ancient holy warrior come (again) as a clownish muscle-bound boaster, bulking up for the

and unprovoked invasion. The millennial machismo threw itself upon
the planet. The profits for its corporations have been, well, orgiastic,
almost miraculous—they can't stop *coming*.

What Lee Quinby calls "apocalyptic masculinity" may be good for
big business. It does not bode well for the peaceable kingdom. In the
face of such monstrous masculinities, feminists may repudiate the
whole range of covert and overt apocalypse, from those who with pious
passion calculate dispensationalist endtimes to those who cold-blood-
edly calculate corporate profits. No wonder Quinby has declared a
feminist "anti-apocalypse"![2] She unveils very precise archaeologies of
the good/evil and male/female dualisms at play in North American
Christian and political life. But without her sort of specific exploration of the apocalyptic tradition, feminism may fall into an anti-apocalyptic dissociation from the biblical prophetic paradigm. Without an
engaged critique, anti-apocalypse may be tempted by a self-deceptive
ms.calculation.

At a certain historical angle, the apocalyptic Other turns out to be
inseparable from the feminist self. Disinterested distance collapses,
for instance, in an analysis of the origins of the women's movement.
Nineteenth-century millennialist themes permeate, indeed in part
produce, the hope and the rhetoric of the "New Woman." This feminist apocalypse is itself readily pushed to the margins of the movement and forgotten. But then it returns (like a woman scorned) with a
vengeance. I find it more promising to read the dreams than to repress
them. We must then recognize in the feminist vision—which has after
all done as much as any movement in history to reshape the world and
even the church—a peculiar apocalyptic mirror-play. Perhaps, if we
keep it in play, the mirroring is liberated into parody, into the sort of
ironic mimesis practiced by the French feminist theorist Luce Irigaray—to whose messianic moment we turn in the end.

Femme du Siècle

Early in my work on apocalypse—as master text and historicized context of all western theopolitics—I had intended a rather straightforward exposé of the self-fulfilling apocalypse prevalent in the nuclear/
ecological/gender politics of the 1980s. But soon I recognized a

strange logic at work. The more strident the opposition to Christian (apocalyptic) ideology—as in such paradigmatic cases as the Marxist metanarrative and, more to the present point, the work of philosopher Mary Daly—the more irresistibly the discourse takes on the demonizing dualism of apocalypse itself: the hope against every other calculable hope, the righteous rage for justice, the purity of a community of martyrs, the impatient hope for a qualitatively and materially transformed future, soon and very soon. Blasting the so-called First Coming of Christian theology "as an absolutizing of men," Daly proposed an anti-apocalyptic "overcoming of dichotomous sex stereotyping, which is the source of the absolutizing process itself." That is surely in part the case. But note the apocalyptic terms of this overcoming: "This event, still on its way, will mean the end of phallic morality. Should it not occur, we may witness the end of the human species on this planet." That may also be. Yet her prediction takes the form of a precise anti-apocalypse: "Seen from this perspective the Antichrist and the Second Coming of women are synonymous."[3] Her own perspective mirrors in reverse the binarism of the apocalypse, yet it was deliberate, parodic in its "reversal of the reversals." This is early second-wave feminism, its satiric anti-absolutes now commanding, after the *fin de millennium* drive to purge feminism of essentialism (of which Daly is the usual suspect), little loyalty. Daly stands in the long—and richly apocalyptic—tradition of her "revolting hags." She might not appreciate such a genealogy. Yet I think it allows us to resist any dismissal of her work and that of other irascibly indispensable prophets.

As though anticipating Daly's discourse over a century earlier, a young French proletarian activist named Claire Demar wrote, "The word of the woman redeemer will be a supremely revolting word." It will be "the broadest, and consequently the most satisfying to every [sexual] nature, to every humor." Demar evoked "the Mother with her thousand voices" embodied in all women as a principle of resistance to masculine repression.[4] Demar and the proletarian women's journal, the fledgling *Tribune,* had appeared in the margins of the Saint-Simonian community, a millennialist movement led by the charismatic Enfantin. Such utopian movements, like the Oneida community or Winstanley's earlier Diggers, prepared the way for Marxist socialism. Far from atheistic, however, they were apocalyptic millennialists, unfolding the utopian prophecies of the eleventh-century visionary Joachim of Fiore. They envisioned a gender egalitarianism

far-fetched for their times, encoded in the "woman clothed with the   57
sun" of Revelation 12 loosely fused with the New Jerusalem. As Demar
soon learned, however, the male leaders preferred their own fantasy
of "the Mother" or "Lady Wisdom" to the work of the journal and of
its living women.[5]

It took female-led utopias to resist—from *within* the codes of apocalypse—the tug of apocalyptic masculinity. For instance, the apocalyptic millennialist movement of the Shakers, led by Ann Lee, who
herself became identified by her followers as the Wisdom figure of
Revelation 12, maintained a fascinating hybrid of gender egalitarianism and apocalyptic revolt. For the trinitarian pattern of Joachite
third-age millennialism it has substituted the radical concept of the
Divine Couple, "the Mother/Father God." An extraordinary Shaker
ditty identifies the age of the Antichrist, extending from the onset
of orthodox imperial Christendom to her time, with the trinitarian
hegemony:

> The monstrous beast, and bloody whore
> Reign'd thirteen hundred years and more;
> and under foot the truth was trod,
> By their mysterious threefold God:
> But while they placed in the *He*
> Their sacred co-eternal *Three*,
> A righteous persecuted few
> Ador'd the everlasting *Two*.[6]

Thus is already lampooned what Daly would eventually mock as the cosmic Boys' Club, the ultimate symbol of male bonding. The apocalypse
code is deployed freely, with the prophetic authority of a community
of prophetic martyrs, against the arch patriarchy of the church—and
of course of the canonical apocalypse.

One can then follow rather precisely the increasing political force
of feminist millennialist rhetoric. The Methodist Frances Willard, one
of the most prominent public female voices of the late nineteenth
century, announced "the coming reign of God and of woman." The
theopolitics of this eschatology is manifest: "She will come into government and purify it, into politics and cleanse [it] . . . for woman
will make home-like every place she enters, and she will enter every
place on this round earth."[7] Essentialist, indeed—let she who is without essences cast the first stone! Even as such prophecy finds no reli-

gious home, it remains a spiritual discourse. In 1881 Matilda Joslyn Gage wrote that "the male element has thus far held high carnival, crushing out all the divine elements of human nature. . . . The recent disorganization of society warns us that in the disenfranchisement of woman we have let loose the reins of violence and ruin which she only has the power to avert. . . . *All writers recognize women as the great harmonizing elements of the 'new era.'*"[8] A melodramatic moment of this spreading enthusiasm was recorded as a toast at the Illinois Women's Press Association, a bastion of New Womanhood, in 1891:

> Pealing! The clock of Time has struck the woman's hour,
> We hear it on our knees.
> All crimes shall cease, and ancient wrongs shall fail;
> Justice returning lifts aloft her scales,
> Peace o'er the world her olive wants extends,
> And white-robed Innocence from Heaven descends.[9]

The New Jerusalem here descending as an enlightening "Innocence" suggests the virginal (and of course white) purity of an apocalyptic essentialism to which the women's movement remains indelibly indebted. Feminism may, through the challenge of its internal diversities and of a relativizing postmodernism, have outgrown its heritage of all-or-nothing utopian absolutes. But how would it do so—absolutely? Feminist anti-essentialism—with its sister oppositionalism, anti-apocalypse—remains an academic privilege earned by these pitched apocalyptic struggles. But it only lurches toward dishonesty when we forget the mother of all oppositionalisms, the apocalyptic heritage fueling our own righteous rhetoric.

Women inside Apocalypse

Given the strong contribution of a feminist anti-apocalypse, I have needed to reveal a bit of the apocalypse hidden in feminism. The mirror-play of course does not cease just because it is seen. Perhaps it permits a wider refraction, a concave mirror like Irigaray's epistemic speculum, belying any easy distinction between (apocalyptic) other and (anti-apocalyptic) self. Indeed Quinby staged her *Millennial Seductions* as "skeptical revelations of an American feminist on Patmos"—

opposition.

If the opposition of feminism to apocalypticism seems at first absolute, it is not because we unconditionally oppose a biblical text as such. But our culture still deploys those devastating dualisms that merge any excessive female desire with the demonic figure—all-consuming, all-consumed—of the Great Whore. John of Patmos's hysterical denunciation of his female competitor as "Jezebel" was harmless enough in its context. But due to the success of his letter to the churches, its sexist rhetoric has provided an indelible template for his fans. They have practiced such various readings as the polygamous and gynocidal terror of Jan Bockelson's sixteenth-century "New Jerusalem" community, fundamentalism's founding inscription of the nineteenth-century New Woman as "silly women of the last days," and David Koresh's harem. One is struck by the utility of sexism as an engine of empowerment for socially marginalized male believers. Apocalypse has promoted an ascetic, heroic, and dominating masculinity that energizes resistance to a perceived (and often real) oppression and that fuels revolutionary flames. It can declare the New Woman, or feminism, or for that matter any opponent (popes, enemy empires, Manhattan) the Whore of Babylon, and it can do so with a purity of rage unavailable to the compromised Christian mainstream.

In Revelation itself, women are offered three representational options, amid a much wider and more interesting array of masculine types: whore, mother, virgin. There is the *whore in power*, who has a human manifestation in Jezebel, the infamous name John lends his apparent female competitor—perhaps a prophetic leader—in the community of Thyatira (Rev. 2:20-23), and who has the dramatic allegorical form of Babylon the Great, the Great Whore—"for all the nations have drunk of the wine of the wrath of her fornication" (Rev. 18:3). There is the *mother in agony* of Revelation 12, the "woman clothed in the sun" who gives birth in torment, only to have her son whisked direct from the womb up to the Father for safekeeping, while her cosmic radiance fades fast to desert exile. And of course there is the *virgin in the end*, bride of the Lamb, the New Jerusalem herself, as perfect urban anti-type to the wickedness of Rome/Babylon.

A theopolitical paradox kicks in there, in the binary of the two feminized cities. For the Whore of Babylon symbolizes in its context imperial injustice, with its transnational market of luxury goods for Rome and its elite intermediaries. So liberation and third-world Christians have found in this text a stunning solidarity with the plight of the oppressed.[10] For instance, liberation theologian Nestor Miguez's exegesis of the Whore of Babylon deploys the rhetorical power of apocalypse to expose the empire of late capitalist global economics. In Revelation the global trade in luxury items is portrayed as obscene (hence the lengthy diatribe against the merchants and the sea captains, by which Roman trade and rule extended throughout the known world); thus, such an economic hermeneutics as Miguez's seems fitting and effective.[11] "Babylon . . . stands for whatever system enthrones the marketplace . . . , for whatever turns the human body and soul into merchandise for trade. Within such a system the only need that exists is the need of those who have the ability to pay; consequently the basic needs of all human beings yield to the luxury markets of great merchants and traders." Martyrdom then can be read not as addiction to butchery, but as an inevitable consequence of subversion: "As in the case of John, the system condemns those who expose the fetishistic nature of the marketplace."[12]

The "apocalyptic hermeneutic" stands in intertextual fidelity to the western revolutionary tradition. As Ernst Bloch has argued in *The Principle of Hope*, this tradition derives its radical futurity, its utopian hope for the fullness of justice for the poor, from the revived medieval apocalyptic tradition that runs from Joachim of Fiore through the Radical Franciscans to the Radical Reformation. Thus, some feminist scholars, seeking (as feminism surely needs to do) to strengthen the bonds of solidarity with liberation movements based on economic, class, and race analysis, defend it fiercely. These advocates mirror its righteousness assertively, as part of what I have called the liberation *neo-apocalypse*. Elisabeth Schüssler Fiorenza especially has called feminists to task for their dismissals of John's Apocalypse; she designates it the sole book of the New Testament wholly devoted to justice.[13] Of course the simplistic oppositionalism of the apocalyptic rhetoric threatens to take possession of every such liberation neo-apocalypse, thus reinscribing the absolutism that funds sexism (and as Daly absolutely insists, vice versa).

Indeed, from the liberation point of view, which focuses on the power of "comfort and protest" this text affords the oppressed, it is surprising that the Book of Revelation made it into the canon. Augustine of Hippo, ensconced as a bishop within the new Christian empire

elitist tones against those chiliasts who read it literally. Yet he seemed
less concerned with heading off a proto-fundamentalism than defus-
ing its disorderly, indeed, revolutionary implications for history. His
insistence that the millennium has already come with the triumph of
the church in the newly Christianized Roman empire meant for him
that there could be nothing qualitatively better within history. This
triumphalism (without Augustine's own critical reserve) would be
solidified as the basis for all orthodox Christian eschatology and the
basis for the constitutive *anti-apocalypse* of the western mainstream.

But the imperial center has turned systematically toward its apocalyptic margin nonetheless, seducing the combustible mythos toward
anti-revolutionary ends. Thus it has emulated Augustine's emphasis
upon the final judgment and a hell for the disobedient (he argues
in exquisite detail for the miraculous new creation of bodies capable
of burning eternally in torment). Thus mainstream Christianity, for
all its anti-apocalyptic defenses, strengthened itself with the vision
so foreign to most of the Hebrew and Christian scriptures, of a holy,
messianic masculinity ennobling itself before the spectacle of the
stripped whore and all her lovers burning in naked agony. In other
words, the conservative anti-apocalypse of classical Christianity has
supported an apocalyptic underside, a hell-belly. It has reflected and
absorbed the apocalypse in ways Euro-American feminist scholars
and other de-apocalypticizing critics may find themselves mirroring:
damning [14] the damners, demonizing the demonizers, excluding the
excluders.

Hegemonic secular modernity has repeatedly renewed itself by
reabsorbing apocalypse, as well, and indeed from its own originative "new world." Take for example the surprising—and traditionally
repressed—testimony of Christopher Columbus as to his own apocalyptic self-identity: "Of the New Heaven and Earth which our Lord
made, as St. John writes in the Apocalypse, after He had spoken it by
the mouth of Isaiah, He made me the messenger thereof and showed
me where to go."[15] I have elsewhere excavated the gendered morphol-
ogy with which he envisioned this paradise as *breast*. An old tradition
of the lost Eden, merging terrestrial paradise with apocalyptic hope,
was sucked at this critical moment in history into a new and aggressive
literalism. The fruits of his inspiration literally funded and founded
the *otra mondo*—the "other world," later dubbed "new world." "Revela-

tion" from above became "discovery" from afar. The apocalyptic realization of crusading warrior masculinity is now consolidated under the banners of early modernity: cross, commerce, and conquest. The dark Other, defeated or else damned, would henceforth serve as the apocalyptic teat of a series of western empires, manfully sucking the planet dry.

Babylonian Bite

Attention to our own varying standpoints *within* the story of apocalypse might not damn our ongoing efforts to transmute power. Rather it allows us to study and so to interrupt the "apocalypse habit." The point would be not to purify our discourse of all apocalyptic elements. For every purge reinscribes apocalypse. The point would be instead (in something like Vipassana Buddhist style) to watch them arise. In every emergency—personal and collective—we may notice the code of victimized righteousness versus absolute evil, of fascinated expectation of total destruction, the yearning for a utopian that is no possible place. Might we practice a kind of *eschatological attentiveness* ("wake, for it comes like the thief in the night"), attention *to and through* apocalypse? Would this allow us to make the necessary discernments of right and wrong—while avoiding final judgment? Disrupting the grim gaze of a warrior-judge upon ourselves or any others? Might the irony of a *counter-apocalypse* de-center the pattern in its religious and secular, sexist and feminist forms?

Parody may lend a lightening touch. Such humor has surfaced, for instance, in the satiric feminism of Susan Smith Nash's *Channel-Surfing the Apocalypse*, inspired by the endtime experience in her home, Oklahoma City. That terror had been inspired by a telling blend of white supremacist millennialism, the gun cult, a pilgrimage to Waco, and the frustration of Timothy McVeigh, a veteran of the Gulf War, that Bush Sr. had not gone in after Saddam Hussein. (Too bad McVeigh couldn't hold on until the like-minded Jr. was elected.) Baghdad/Babylon has beckoned across the millennia. "The bombing. A warning sign that something is wrong. Which myth do you prefer in the quest to explain it? Apocalyptic? Utopian? Evolutionary? Historical? Chaos theory?"[16] In a vignette called "Signs That the End Is Near (If Anyone Still Cares . . .)" she fantasizes shopping in the mall, where she sees a mannequin dressed in a seductive gypsy costume.

> You do not realize that it is a statue of "The Great Harlot" who sits
> on a seven-headed scarlet-colored beast, and you do not see what is
> tattooed on her forehead: MYSTERY, BABYLON THE GREAT, THE
> MOTHER OF HARLOTS AND ABOMINATIONS OF THE EARTH.
> You like the ensemble, so you try it on. It's a purple and scarlet dress,
> bedecked with gold and precious stones. . . . As you try on the dress
> you feel a strange transformation.

A man on the escalator comes on to her offensively. She grows fangs.
I'll leave to the reader's imagination what happens to the offender. In
her, uh, biting parody of lurid fundamentalist depictions of the Great
Whore, Nash temporarily defangs the grim misogyny of the book. She
inhabits a geography in which the text of Revelation is never silent.

With perhaps less bite and more chew, I too have "tried on" the feminine apocalyptic personae. I found myself writing little stories about
them. For the sake of a counter-apocalypse I found myself befriending
the woman trapped within the man-made Great Whore. I found in
her a fleshy powerflirt, Babs, who by the end of the second Christian
millennium had entered into a conspiracy (a "breathing together")
with Jeri (alias New Jerusalem) and Sophia, the long-suffering sun-
woman of Revelation 12, who had gained considerable earth-centered
wisdom during her desert retreat.[17]

The Incalculable Present

Luce Irigaray wrote, "These prophets feel that, if something divine
can still come to us, it will do so when we abandon all calculation. . . .
These predecessors have no future—they come from it. Within them,
it is already present. But who hears it? Obscurely their song waters the
world. Of today, of yesterday, of tomorrow."[18] Can something divine
still come to us? If not, our theopolitics devolves into mere ideology.
Shall we follow Irigaray's admonition to "abandon all calculation"?
Can we cut free of every endtime calculus, every deadline, every dead-
ening prediction of the end of the world, every profitable calculation
of outcomes? Chaos theory does indeed suggest a nonlinear temporality, not a circularity without newness, but the new that cannot be
predicted. Yet this invitation to abandon calculation, to leap beyond
the safety nets of certainty, does not leap beyond the apocalypse. Like
Derrida's "messianicity without a messiah," irrupting from outside of
Christian intention, it trembles with apocalyptic codes. Does this song

of the incalculable echo the purity of the masculinist messianism? Is this another closeted feminist absolute? If so, we would no longer want it, need it, or believe it.

Yet it is Irigaray from whom feminist theory has learned the strategy of a mimetic parody, by way of assertion of gender difference in the face of the sexist Same. So perhaps we may read her eschatological oracles as parodic mimicry of the Christian apocalypse that helps us to unhinge it from its bitter misogyny and its terminal justice, while refreshing again the wilder, wider hope of the world with the dream of living waters, water free and pure for all, melodic, laughing waters. Quite consonant with Jürgen Moltmann's theology of hope, she announces a possibility that does not follow the line that can be extrapolated from the present but rather comes from the future, comes even now. Does this eschatology not echo the New Testament promise of *ho erchomenos*, "The One Who Comes"? Indeed, as though instinctively, with no commentary and no reference to the history of apocalypticism, even biblical, she grasps the thousand-year-old Joachite vision of the third aeon, giving it a feminist face: she announces the opening of "the third era" of "the couple," "the Spirit and the Bride." This is a reference to Rev. 21:17: "The Spirit and the Bride say, 'Come.'"

Irigaray may have been thinking in terms of the dyad of her "ethic of sexual difference."[19] The Spirit is no groom, however. The Spirit blows where it will—into any or no sex, with any and all partners. The Bride of the Spirit suggests an open female subjectivity, a disclosing subjectivity. She comes from the future and transforms the shame of the past into tensive paradoxes. She has always been coming. The open signifying field of her gender, her sex, does not make her any less female. The problems of history, the terrors of empire—her advent will not solve them. But they will not be solved without her.

In a two-thousand-year-old wisdom papyrus, some anonymous prophet gathered together the shards and voices of women into a great "I AM." She sings right to us. From its past the future still comes, the subject of an incalculable present tense. This self-revealing I is a mimicry and a metamorphosis of every once-for-all, one-and-only word, every final apocalypse:

> I am the first and the last.
> I am the honored one and the scorned one.
> I am the whore and the holy one. I am the wife and the virgin.

I am the mother and the daughter. . . .
I am the voice whose sound is manifold
and the word whose appearance is multiple.[20]

5

Eyes All Over:
Liberation and Deconstruction

> Around the throne . . . are four living creatures, full of eyes in front and behind: the first . . . like a lion, the second . . . like an ox, the third . . . with a face like a human face, and the fourth . . . like a flying eagle. And the four living creatures, each of them with six wings, are full of eyes all around and inside. Day and night without ceasing they sing.
>
> —Revelation 4:6-8

The four creatures arrayed around the bejeweled, shining, flashing, thundering throne, standing on "something like a sea of glass, like crystal," return the glitter with open eyes, mirroring back the lightening glories of the deity. John of Patmos displays the highest destination of Jewish mystical apocalypticism, the divine throne room, as surrounded by the four mythic creatures (*Chayyot*) driving Ezekiel's fiery chariot of half a millennium prior. But while Ezekiel had spread only the rim of the wheels with ocular organs, John outdoes him. The creatures "are full of eyes all around and inside." He saturates the creatures' bodies with eyes. And so has John's vision of visions saturated the body of Christ—its churches, its cultures, its countercultures—with its multiplicity of views, not with a single one.

Nor has there been a single authoritative interpretation of the Christian Apocalypse, let alone of its force field of effects. So this astonishing image, full of eyes, gives us an opportunity to reflect upon the multiple strategies available to us for reading and engaging the apocalyptic legacy. We have been considering a variety of counter-imperial and feminist lenses for a theopolitical optic. In this chapter we will take the opportunity to scan the hermeneutical spectrum of apocalyptic readings. The tensions between liberation theology and a postmodern, poststructuralist reading now come into play. They are reflected in the contrasts between different styles of feminist herme-neutics. Yet if we attend to the playful polyoptics of the four creatures, if we read the text as dream and read the dream as our own, these tensions need not leave us divided against ourselves. The tensions of multiple visions may hold open a space in which together we face our fears and activate our hopes.

Vision within the vision, vision of visions: eyes proliferate over the four bodily surfaces, eyes line their innards, merging inside and out, day and night. Already in Ezekiel these creatures disorder the divi-sions of human, animal, angel, and monster. In John they break into polyoptic perversity. The android—"like a human face"—offers no familiar point of view, no humanistic privilege. He blends into har-mony within a classification of animals, merely the third member of the animal quartet that relentlessly sings and stares. Do these eyes ever blink? Do they portend the nightless neon of the final day? Then, in the culminating biblical trope of total Presence, the One on the throne will replace the sun and shine continuously. Do these omni-ocular bodies not prepare the way for the single, eternally switched-on Lamb-Lamp (Rev. 22:3-5)? Certainly they never sleep. They are wakefulness itself. Watch—it comes in the twinkling of an eye. The apocalypse. *The Apocalypse.* Keep your eyes open.

Or at least the book. Could we close it by now even if we tried, as have so many? A casual sampling: "My spirit cannot abide this text" —Martin Luther; "ravings of a lunatic"—Thomas Jefferson; "a curi-ous record of the vision of a drug addict"—George Bernard Shaw; "repellant because it resounds with the dangerous snarl of the frus-trated, suppressed collective self, the frustrated power-spirit in man, vengeful"—D. H. Lawrence; "there are many monsters in the Apoc-alypse, but the real bad-ass monster sits on the heavenly throne" —Tina Pippin;[1] "congested with vision . . . a postmodern monstros-ity"—Catherine Keller.[2]

down the hyperspeed of John's vision, flashing like MTV to the next image, and the next, and—his sentences are grammatically gorged with "and"—the images multiply like the eyes. Something in this text keeps winking at me, something still trying, for all the hallucinogenic overexposure of the Apocalypse, to get some attention. Pssst, here, look. Within this proof text of the most exclusively, the most fundamentally singular gaze, might these creatures be silently sending signals invisible to the author himself? In their eye-studded bodies might they signify multiplicity itself—quite precisely the endless plurality of viewpoints? This would be a poignant condition, given their context. What views of the Apocalypse itself would such plurivision open up? What views of its legacy of exclusive, once-for-all, all-for-One, one and only truth claims? If we (postmodern by default or by desire) gaze into the ancient kaleidoscope of this text, do we see anything but eyes eyeing us? How many of them are our own mirrored back?

Deconstructing the Book

I raise these questions this way to try to demonstrate, not merely to adumbrate, a style of reading that proceeds for now under the cover of the "postmodern." It might pass as a response to David Tracy's recent call for theology to heal the split between its form and its content. Rather than mobilizing another methodological apparatus, or recapitulating the work of Apocalypse commentaries (which proliferated at the millennium like the eyes), rather than "arguing the apocalypse"[3] within the rapidly fading context of the millennium, rather even than developing my own categories of anti-apocalypse, retro-apocalypse, neo-apocalypse, counter-apocalypse, I am staging a hermeneutical encounter with its four creatures.

Such an encounter cannot take place without borrowing the poetic license with which these chauffeur-creatures first operated. But then I would make the same claim about theology in general: it cannot encounter its originating texts unless it enters into the form, not merely into an abstraction of the content, of the artful imagery of scripture. To the extent that theology has instead merely extracted a supposed "biblical" meaning, it has practiced a hermeneutic of control. The alternative is not to be controlled by the text. If we seek instead a theological hermeneutic of relation, that is, of indeterminacy—influenced by the model of quantum theory, in which the relation of observer and observed evinces an uncontrollable and irreducible mutuality—it is not in the rather transparently self-authorizing guise of merely subordinating ourselves to the text.

This hermeneutical indeterminacy admits at once its kinship to deconstruction. That is, it presumes that the rhetorical constructs of Revelation reveal much more about its writers and readers than about any One sitting on a throne. I assume that Derrida's poorly understood slogan, *"pas de hors texte"* (nothing outside the text), illumines the way in which we are always already in this text—in apocalypse, in its tone, in its force field of effects, its culture, its aftermath.[4] Yet such an intra-apocalyptic position might lock us into a temporality that dissolves every moment into a prelude to the end, which was framed by an author who certainly intended to capture all time and space within the net of his text. "Nothing outside of the text": no exit? Yet the end does not come but continuously generates new beginnings, which rush toward it. And what closure does such a text threaten or promise that does not dissolve into relativity as we approach it? The end of death, of time, of history, the end of the Roman church, the end of the aristocracy, the end of the bourgeoisie, the end of patriarchy—which single goal stands still, stands there as "The End," the final goalpost, outpost of all known perspectives? Or am I asking *merely* postmodern questions, meaninglessly multiplicative, not yet interpretative, a "post" signifying that there is no significance?

One writes—now—about Apocalypse post-millennium, with a redoubled sense of posteriority, of post-apocalypse. Yet commentators on John's Apocalypse have always been constrained by the grammar of a peculiar afterward, by the throne room temporality of that future that John witnessed (*martyrein*) in advance, as though the future lay already in the past: "And I saw a star that had fallen from heaven to earth." Interpretation takes place always as afterword, in the afterward of a perpetual not yet, not quite, soon, and very soon.

How would we step altogether outside of the agonized time pretzel of apocalypticized western history? Perhaps we return to the text—the text of no return, of pure destruction and New Creation—in order to discern the trace of an alternative spacetime, of a disclosure even here in this revelation of ultimate closure. The term *trace* here echoes

Derrida's sense of the difference (French: *differance*) that haunts the same, which defers closure. "Without a retention in the minimal unit of temporal experience, without a trace retaining the other as other in the same, no difference would do its work and no meaning would appear."[5] The Derridian *differance* still (unlike many of its adherents) insists upon "meaning." It does not negate the world in and toward which language signifies. Deconstruction meditates on time, indeed on the spacing of time and the temporizing of space, therefore on a world in which the text lives, a world that it permeates and affects. If there is nothing outside of the text, this is because *no fixed boundary can be drawn between the text and its context,* between, for instance, our texts' interpretation of Ezekiel and later Jewish apocalypses and the history of Christian interpretations of the text and our own late, very late, version of and within that history.

Nonetheless, I do not "apply" Derridian method to the Bible, rendering the text a pretext for poststructuralist performance. It is more accurate to say that prior struggle with this particular text, with all that it protects and ignores and assaults and hopes, all that it closes and discloses, sent me after the fact, after "the book" (too late), to Derrida. This text has done a lot of sending. Its endtime missionaries are everywhere on the planet. Derrida has also sent his postcard (mass mailings to the U.S. academy), further deferring the arrival of the parousia: "Within every sign already, every mark . . . there is distancing, the post, what there has to be so that it is legible for another."[6] It seems then only fair to read the text through one or two Derridian eyes, but then also, inevitably and at the same time, to read Derrida through the eyes of this text. Derrida clarifies precisely what a theologian might need from a deconstructive reading: "Operating necessarily from the inside, borrowing all the strategic and economic resources of subversion from the old structure, borrowing them structurally, that is to say without being able to isolate their elements and atoms, the enterprise of deconstruction always in a certain way falls prey to its own work."[7] Thus we enter a space we have never quite left, beginning on the inside—itself full of eyes. The encounter can only be intimate, therefore, risking proximity to the mythopoetic vortex of the imagery. The encounter cannot then remain bounded within the disciplines of history or literary analysis. The distance collapses along with the familiarity of the canonized text. In other words—admittedly not in the words of the philosopher himself—deconstruction exposes us to the theological force field of the text. Once sucked into its whirl-wind, we may only move gracefully by making intentional theological gestures of our own. Or is that the bias of a theologian?

Only in its apophatic and apocalyptic moments has theology learned to reflect upon how it "falls prey to its own work," how it voices doctrinal certainties only by silencing competitors, how otherwise it dissolves at its own boundaries, how it stutters at the edge of speech. This element of predation should not come as a surprise, given Revelation's cosmic bestiary of predators—animal, divine, demonic—that play their roles within a theater serving as the prototype for western revolution and reaction and arguably already mimicking the structures it subverts. Deconstruction recognizes that it operates always within its text, since the text has no final boundaries. Such an interior position eschews any parasitical spirit of negation, which would only destroy its own host.[8] It is also the case that in all of its forms theology (in distinction from other religious studies, perhaps even biblical studies) presup-poses and cultivates this interiority. It may defend violently or rigidly against all deconstructive gestures, but it at least recognizes that it operates always within a tradition and a community derived from the interpretation of a text. The text of texts, to be sure—whose status as the canonized and closed Book surely inspired the Derridian call for "The End of the Book and the Beginning of Writing."[9]

Reentering the book of books, indeed the Book of the End, we may find ourselves, however unpleasantly, already mirrored, refracted, seen—rewritten. We may not emerge with critical singularity of vision, with a monoperspectival clarity "about" it, as though we had finally gotten outside of it and could look on. I hope we can read without either the aching apologetics of most progressive Christianity, strain-ing its good news from Revelation's toxins, or the seamless sarcasm of a particular tone of deconstruction, for which good news is no news. I have found serviceable instead (as a feminist theologian, who can-not afford the luxuries of justification or of dismissal) a certain meth-odological ambivalence. According to this hermeneutical uncertainty principle, our relativity as interpreters enmeshed in an endless pro-cess of interpretation—Nietzsche's "infinite interpretation"—does not absolve us of specific ethical and ecological responsibilities. Rather it holds us accountable to definite relations to and within our world. In other words, it always obliges itself to a constructive re-vision.

Returning to the text, we find that, of the four "living creatures," the eagle and the lion represent beasts of prey, sated here by the vision of God. The third, the humanoid, represents the most aggressive preda- tor on the planet, the one who has posed its culture against nature. The ox, a creation of domestication, pulls the weight of human cul- ture. The four pray (sing) continuously, engorged with eyes, eyes that we might imagine look out pitilessly, blankly, like royal Assyr- ian statuary. Or do they strain, bloodshot, with infinite insomnia? or gaze in hallucinogenic hallelujah at what is forbidden to human eyes? We see these eyes seeing. Unlike the eye of God, which sees but is not seen, these eyes are spread out before our vision, through John's vision, mirroring his mystical throne-room voyeurism back to him, to us, in an endless—if textually fleeting—refraction. Unlike the single point of view, the God's-eye view that is therefore no point of view but mere omniscience, these eyes would appear to stare back at us in extravagant multiplicity. Traditionally the covering of divine beings or demons with eyes connoted their inhuman vision, their omnivorous sight, their all-seeing and all-knowing consciousness or if not know-it- all—most commentaries reserve omniscience for the deity, with whom they do not want to identify these creatures—at least their inescapable attention. We cannot see what the eyes see, and the eye-bearers are eternally singing. So one cannot read the text as an uncharacteris- tically Hellenistic privilege of vision over audition, as dispassionate speculation. Rather it offers the tableau of a harmoniously monstrous little menagerie, day and night singing their *Sanctus*.

Still, Revelation makes quite a spectacle of itself. What are we to say back to the philosopher Friedrich Nietzsche when he, tormented prophet against Christian cruelty, cites at length Tertullian's prom- ise? For our present purpose, gazing at Tertullian's vision through Nietzsche's furiously apostate eye seems all too appropriate:

> "We have martyrs instead of athletes. If we crave blood, we have the
> blood of Christ. . . . But think what awaits us on the day of his tri-
> umph!" And the rapt visionary continues: "Yes, and there are still to
> come other spectacles—that last, that eternal Day of Judgment, that
> Day which the Gentiles never believed would come, . . . when this
> old world and all its generations shall be consumed in one fire. How

vast the spectacle that day, and how wide! What sight shall wake my wonder." . . . *Per fidem*: so it is written.[10]

Perhaps one can say back: the power of Nietzsche's fiery denunciation emanates from his mimesis of the apocalyptic tone. When he later dubs himself Antichrist, he surely reveals his own implication in its reverberating intertextuality. The choice of Zarathustra, a reference to Zoroaster, the likeliest candidate for progenitor of all apocalyptic discourse, reflects the mirroring of many ancient eyes.[11] Infinite interpretation. After The Book.

"Anyone whose name was not found written in the book of life was thrown into the lake of fire" (Rev. 20:15). Christians have lived by the hope that their names have been inscribed in that final book, reservations in the splendid New Jerusalem confirmed. Progressive Christianity of course wants the hope without the hell. We invoke the social architecture of the New Creation without the torture chambers in the basement—liberation without the final exteriorization of our particular oppressors, our Other, as damned or demon, justice for the Others of history, not vengeance. Indeed I can no longer deny solidarity with certain aspects of this text—its wish for "no more tears," for "water free for all," hopes desperately dear to the growing majority of the present earth.

Yet to claim the liberating without the damning seems perilous: Do we not then "take away from the words of the book of this prophecy"? If so, "God will take away his share in the tree of life and in the holy city, which are described in this book." Our selective readings had better make their ambivalence clear, had better admit when they read against the grain of the text, had better thus relativize the authority of this author to the moral claims of variously oppressed publics. Some of these publics read it, hope and pray through it; masses of others will remain outside of Christianity, if not outside its effects. Thus if we do not want to transmit the greatest binary closure in all literature, if we do not want to absorb the damnation along with the salvation, liberation hermeneutics may wish to consider admitting the moral limits of this book—even and especially while recognizing the virtual illimitability of its effects: *nothing outside the text*.

This book of books, indeed, makes a spectacle of scrolls, of text, of itself *as* book, of its own bookishness. *Text* after all distinguishes itself from *voice* by virtue of its visibility. John is writing feverishly at the

angel's command, of course, and along the way swallows a book—tex- 75
tuality itself?—whole: "bitter to your stomach, but sweet as honey in
your mouth." Any postmodernism that joins Derrida in privileging the
text over orality should recognize its risky continuity with John's Book,
whose preoccupation with writing is unprecedented in the Bible. Far
be it from the present writer to suggest any link between writing and
hell. But when we celebrate the sweetness of "writing"—indeed Derrida set a "pure writing" apart from the logocentric authority of voice
and book—we may want to remember the Apocalypse. "Write!" com-
mands the angel, indeed, "in a book," the ultimate in closure. Yet the
operative contrast in Revelation is not between book and text, but
between speech and writing.[12]

We may wish to recall the bitter belly and the unprecedented hell
that accompany this early assertion of the privilege of writing. With
its hell, it at once disposes of its Others and reinscribes them in its
margins. John's vision of the new creation requires that the damned
pile up against the gates of the holy city, even in the end. Perhaps this
irresolvable divide communicates that the New Jerusalem—in which
trees produce leaves "for the healing of the nations"—after all does
not stand outside of history, outside of struggle and opposition. Yet
the bitter, damning rage does not even aspire toward a wider redemption, let alone a salvation of the whole. Like Jonah before the whale,
the concept of God still trying to redeem the idolaters remains intol-
erable to John. The sweetness of salvation is textually enhanced by the
contrasting hell. Writing may be a bitter pill, but it promises the final
healing.

The surface of the New Jerusalem sparkles with myriad gems. In
its architecture of pure culture, the natural elements reappear as
park, purged of all wilderness—rivers are canals; trees are planted
in geometries, yielding useful fruits. The sun has no more use; "there
will be no more sea." In my own affinity to poststructuralist projects
of "denaturalization," I cannot miss the apocalyptic anticipation of
the radical denaturalization of the universe, in which the elements
are melted down as in a cosmic forge: the primordial chaos, waste
and wild, the predatory animals, the wild bodies, have no place at all
in this apotheosis of pure culture. As temple complex it magnifies,
indeed it now in some sense takes the place of, the glittering throne of
God, who will in the end inhabit his creation fully. Yet only the Lamb,
most domesticated of all creatures, appears in that end, shining as

the twenty-four-hour lamp of the pure light of YHWH. A tired set of neon-blasted eyes might read here the worst of the postmodern, the Dysney-topia of pure artifice.

Animal Dreams

Our beastly quartet, however, stands a bit to the side of all this horror and hope. They have seen it all. And perhaps because they stand off, seeing too much, seeing from innumerable perspectives, they were adopted as the supreme mascots of textuality. Through patristic allegory they were typologized as the four Gospels. If there is "good news" for postmodernity in this textual polyoptics, it lies in the unlikely ancient protection of an irreducible plurality: for all the massive subsequent success of the Christian imperial mononarrative, the multiplicity of perspectives itself got fixed within its canon. (Psst: look, not two eyes and a single view, not a single story, not a single Gospel.) The need for four, still dangling their loose ends and mutual contradictions, rather than a compression into one, remains neither trivial nor explicable. Indeed, under the circumstances of an aggressively domesticated and monocultured Christianity, it remains a little wild.

And how hungrily the visual artists of the Middle Ages would pounce on this little bestiary. In this exegesis I find myself standing with one foot in this nonlinguistic subculture, within a long lineage of anonymous iconographers grateful for this animating animality. Authorized to lift these four supreme authors into relief from the text, the sculptor of a tympanum on a cathedral could slow the vision down to granite. Celtic manuscript illuminators caressed and complicated these images, enmeshing them in twining beasts and vines, bringing their own ancient cosmological symbolism to new fruition as it reframed the missionary culture of the Book. I easily project myself into their eyes: into the visual artists' and their people's appetite for all that could be saved from the new dualism of God as the supernatural, the church as the pure culture of the Logos: the elemental presences, the creaturely images, wild things, monsters, gargoyles; indeed even lambs, Mary, the baby. Anything but more men, more beards, more stiffened desensualized bodies. Anything for relief from the droning, dematerialized andromorphism and anthropomorphism—which was after all hardly getting off the ground in the rich sensorium of the

the first creation its chance. (As I said, I project.)

Scholars recognize a "capacity to see, which vastly exceeds the human."[13] The Revelation commentary by Catherine González and Justo González, which is oriented to social justice, joins in this old tradition of hungry hermeneutics, reaching for support into the more flesh-friendly Jewish tradition: "These four living creatures probably represent all living beings, for there was a rabbinic tradition that the greatest of wild animals was the lion, the greatest of domestic animals was the ox, the greatest of birds was the eagle, and the greatest of all was the human creature. Thus, the four living creatures bring to the throne the worship of the entire creation."[14] This is a hopeful reading, and I share the hope, if not the reading. Yet even these authors do not, unfortunately, problematize their eco-sensitive exegesis in terms of Revelation's anticipation of virtual geocide as the presupposition for the New Creation. They appropriately link John's new creation to the Isaianic eschatology it cites, but they then simply affirm the new creation as the end of death ("it is eternal life") and as the proper Christian expectation. One might want at least a struggle, an acknowledgment, of some cognitive dissonance between the emerging vision of the end of all mortality and the Jewish eschatological one of a renewal of creation, this creation, in which life cannot be abstracted from death. The failure to acknowledge such biblical tensions illustrates the problem with liberation apologetics mentioned earlier. Moreover, the traditional left's commitment to social justice has until recently been won at the expense of care for nonhuman creatures, who have been fair game for exploitation. Indeed "dominion" (Hebrew: *kabash*, Genesis 1) has been exercised with violent anthropocentrism on both the right and the left sides of Christianity. By the same token it illustrates the rhetorical power of having the Bible on your side in order to advance a progressive agenda, a strategic situation I share. We must beware, however, inadvertently betraying the material context for the vitality both symbolized and embodied in "all living beings."[15]

Neither should I expect sympathy from many poststructuralists for my animalization of text. They are just as likely to have disregarded the nonhuman earth. They are less likely than the biblical writers to include the multiplicity of creatures within paeans to the plural. Indeed postmodernists may anthropomorphize faster than the Apocalypse, anxious to root out the conceptual residues of "nature."

They rightly expose the sort of fixed, conservative, logocentric nature that has been dubbed in where, instead, "culture" should be made to acknowledge its own construction. Yet while culture remains within poststructuralist writing a concept larded with rich complexities, nature is left in the dust of its deconstruction.[16]

I find an intriguing corroboration of my own concern in Derrida's formulation of the "trace": "If the trace, arche-phenomenon of 'memory,' which must be thought before the opposition of nature and culture, animality and humanity, etc., belongs to the very movement of signification then signification is *a priori* written, whether inscribed or not, in one form or another, in a 'sensible' and 'spatial' element that is called 'exterior.'"[17] Here Derrida makes clear that his metaphor of text should not be reduced to any graphic medium, nor read as lacking reference to the material universe. Might we consider the pericope of the four polyoptic, polymorphic creatures to bear just such a trace of the sensible-spatial exterior, in which all living creatures become and pass away? But this exterior has precisely leaked into the text, before it is even written, in such a way as to dissolve the dualisms of nature/culture and animal/human.

"Trace" is equivalent to *differance*, when "differance, in a certain and very strange way, [is] 'older' than the ontological difference or than the truth of Being." When it has this age it can be called the play of the trace."[18] Certainly John's Hebrew throne-room vision, and even his early Christianization of its context, recalls a faith older than its revision by Greek ontological categories. The beasts in their celestial gaminess mark an even older moment, at the very least prior to the conquest of the biblical paradigm by what Martin Heidegger first called "ontotheology"—the identification of God with immutable, self-knowing Being. Their iconographic citation, however, of even older, mythological imagery of the ancient world can hardly be missed. And the ancient Middle East sits on a neolithic understanding of animals, in which the lines between nature and culture, animality and humanity, seem to have been drawn only sufficiently to allow their mutant and hybrid recombinations.

Perhaps the signifying movement of the beasts, precisely as they include a human not as "greatest" but as so pointedly just third of four, marks its difference from the anthropomorphism which had all along been gathering momentum along the biblical trajectory as well. This bestial reading may not seem capricious when linked to other wild traces, such as preeminently the whirlwind epiphany of Job 39–43. That text, if interpreted out of the commentary commonplace of a divine bully declaring supremacy over creation, grants only the untameable bodies of the cosmos and of feral animals the honor of appearing in the restorative creation vision. This whirling, distinctly noneschatological vision undermines the supremacy of the human to great ecological effect.[19] The "carnival of creation" mocks the domesticating anthropocentrism of human cultural presumption.[20] I am not conflating Job with Revelation. On the contrary, everything that YHWH offers as creation from the whirlwind gets eliminated in John's New Creation. Moreover, no purely animal-centric or ecotheological perspective can apply to these or any other biblical beasts. I do wish to register, however, the improbable possibility of an *ecotheologically post-structuralist* set of eyes with which to view or review them. From such perspectives, the consonance of the four animals with Job's vision hints perhaps at most at a residual counter-tradition, which might signify something quite beside the author's point.

Book of Blood

Within a few verses the lens will shift to the supreme beast, the object of this prayer, the Lion of Judah who appears as the Lamb: "The good old lion in sheep's clothing," quips D. H. Lawrence.[21] The Lion-Lamb also has too many eyes—seven, one presumably for each of the seals that he alone is worthy to break, to open and read. He is the predator who has fallen prey, the better . . . to read? He is slaughtered in order to conquer: "By your blood you ransomed . . . ," the gory heart of the coming Christian metanarrative, the predator become prey to whom we pray in hopes of . . . the apocalyptic feast? The book's climactic moments of eating include the consumption of a scroll, the Beasts (unlike our good ones) who "strip and cook and eat" the juicy Whore, and the parodic eucharistic feast for the birds of prey at Armageddon. "Come, gather for the great supper of God, to eat the flesh of kings, the flesh of captains . . . flesh of all, both free and slave, both small and great" (Rev. 19:17-18).

Stephen Moore, who confesses "My Father Was a Butcher," has written:

In truth, however, Jesus' throat was cut from the moment that he first strayed, bleating, into [John's] Gospel: "here is the Lamb of God who taketh away the sin of the world! . . . The next day, Jesus staggers by again, still bleeding profusely [see Rev. 5:6]. . . . The trail leads straight to the cross, which is also a spit, for it is as roast lamb that Jesus must fulfill his destiny (cf. 6:52-57): "How can this man give us his flesh to eat?"[22]

Thus Moore, himself prey to poststructuralism, traces the trail of blood between the Johns. He obstructs any tidy opposition between the loving martyrdom of the Gospels and the butcher shop of the Apocalypse. Through the macabre account of the Maccabee brother's iterative self-sacrifice (Maccabees 2 and 4), through Paul's echoing call to imitate Christ's sufferings, Moore performs a stunning deconstruction of the entire apocalyptically charged pattern of martyrology. Holding his gut (having already autobiographically vomited on the threshold of *God's Gym*), he traces a "mimetic chain, slick with blood," as it "snakes out of the text and seeks to coil itself around the audience."[23]

Of course I am reading deconstruction apocalyptically, or vice versa, which is to say that recoil as we may, we as Christians and westerners have that blood on our hands. And if we are still *in* the text, *in* apocalypse, there is no ready escape from this coiling. Another poststructuralist science critic, Donna Haraway, has captured this interiority nicely, with regard to a particular extension of the living text of the Apocalypse, which she recognizes as such, that is, the technoscientific salvation history narrative of what she likes to call the "second christian millennium." Her wider hermeneutical project, that of a "modest witness," resonates with our exegesis. While she herself does not reflect on the martyriological associations of "witness," the modesty she calls for directly counteracts the ferocious single vision of classical apocalypse: "We might learn to live without the bracing discourses of salvation history. We exist in a sea of powerful stories: . . . but no matter what the One-Eyed Father says, there are many possible structures, not to mention contents, of narration. Changing the stories, in both material and semiotic senses, is a modest intervention worth making."[24] I presume we do indeed wish to change the received metanarrative, indeed the traditional interpretation,

of apocalypse. I presume also that the ambiguity of the grammar
of "changing stories" remains irresolvable: Are we to transform this
story or change to a different one? Many who have not actually dismissed John's text for its vengeful, omnicidal, misogynist potencies
are at least disturbed by the toxicity of its *Wirkungsgeschichte*, indeed
of its *wirkliche Geschichte*, that is, of its hermeneutical effects in history.
This "history of effects" can always be written off as bad interpretations—fundamentalist, dispensationalist, millennialist, crusading,
demonizing, pacifying, Stalinizing, Nazifying, Y2K, Hollywood, and
so forth—not the new age, not the reich, not the utopia John had in
mind! But if for a moment we bracket the clumsy question of whether
we should blame the text itself or only its interpretations for all the
human-made apocalypses of two thousand years of biblical citation,
we may at least agree that the story needs changing. Then perhaps
we can read the deconstructive trope of the many eyes as signaling
inside opposition to "the One-eyed Father."

Moore hopes to free the reader from the snaking blood (an avatar
of the red serpent of Revelation 12?), not to redeem the Bible from its
own effects. To join him in this freedom, must we identify the complex
coil of the biblical text with the straight line of Christian imperial
theology? I hope not. The bloody flesh may have served as pulp for
the Book. But none of it had yet, in either apocalypse or gospel, been
sanitized and wrapped as the sacrificial climax—the Cross—of salvation history. The linearity that originates as the Creation and ends in
the Second Coming and New Creation emerges with, and only with,
the baptism of Hellenistic ontotheology. Far from such a metanarrative, the Revelation can barely even muster a narrative: Schüssler Fiorenza has compared its structure to Sonya Delaunay's multicolored
spiral abstractions—coils of form as well as content.[25] Far from the
coherent salvation history that was cooked up from its raw mythological themes, these are bloody remains, nonrepresentational shreds and
splashes, violent flashes and ephemeral blinks of story. Perhaps for
this reason it has inspired the earnest attempts of generations of pre-
millennialists and millennialists to explicate, in meticulous detail, the
secret linearity of the sequence of dispensations. But for this reason
it also inspires some of us to continue to liberate it from the mononarrative.

Return of Ezekiel's Chariot:
Intertextuality and Mysticism

Does this qualify Revelation as at least an original—the raw, meaty vision, to be processed and packaged by later traditions? We need only to check out the oracles of warning in Ezekiel 1–24 or even just the vision of the first chapter to grasp how unoriginal is, for instance, the theme of the four creatures. Christian commentators tend merely to note the dependency in passing, as though Jewish texts exist to resource the New Testament. Of course biblical authors are all stubbornly premodern in their indifference to individual authorship, to the distinction of original and derivate, of citation and plagiarism. But Ezekiel's chariot vision makes John's version read like a hacked up, butchered, overcooked quote.

Ezekiel elaborates the creatures in a poetically beautiful Hebrew, with the sustained attention of one who has seen something that has riveted him to its every detail. Each of the four creatures has four faces (and only four wings, unlike the six John took from Isaiah)—a multiplication of fours suggesting the self-similar complexity of fractal iteration. These creatures, rather than fixed at the foot of a throne, "darted to and fro, like flashes of lightning." As to the eyes, these are not indiscriminately plastered all over and inside the creatures, but rather cover the rims of the mysterious wheels within wheels—one pair for each—by which the collective animal/human/angel/mechanical hybrid travels in any direction. Indeed, through Haraway we may recognize such a compound of biological and machine intelligence as an early cyborg. No wonder UFO enthusiasts prize such evidence of early terrestrial visitations! But setting aside Ezekiel's aeronautical premonitions, the prophet's more immediate concern lay with the historical cataclysm, which his people were about to suffer in the form of the destruction of Jerusalem by Babylon. John encoded a similar sense of dread before the colonial power of the Roman Empire, with the symbol of Babylon, the Great Whore. Of course Ezekiel actually outdoes and prepares the way for the Book of Revelation in the scale of its raging misogynist imagery, taking mainly the form of tantrums against various "whores," tropes for unfaithful cities.

A postmodern reading recognizes John's use of the fragment left over from Ezekiel's chariot not as secondary but as intertextual. As

Daniel Boyarin deploys Julia Kristeva's concept of the intertext in the interpretation of Jewish midrash, "the text is always made up of a mosaic of conscious and unconscious citation of earlier discourse."[26] So even in Ezekiel we do not have the "original"; his more lively, imaginative chariot drew from Canaanite theophanies and local throne iconographies. Ezekiel's chariot inspired the entire Jewish mystical *Hekhalot* tradition of chariot descent, which merged with Jewish apocalypticism to form another stream of influence for John. Indeed, as the Bible and Culture Collective avers: "deconstruction rejects the notion that the origin (*arche*) whatever its form (the author, God, the signified), should be given any sort of priority; it denies that there is an origin in any substantial sense."[27] Of course such denial of absolute origin emits disturbing theological resonances. It begins to unravel at the literary level the very timeline upon which the master narrative of salvation history has depended.

As Boyarin further suggests, "intertextuality is, in a sense, the way that history, understood as cultural and ideological change and conflict, records itself within textuality."[28] John's recognition of the need for a new rhetoric of theodicy in the face of ongoing persecution, for a public response to a threat experienced as economic, ecological, spiritual, global, certainly deserves the liberation reading it has received so strongly across the world, especially in Latin America and Africa. Like Ezekiel, John faced up to the crushing power of imperial injustice. Ezekiel worked to help his people retain a sense of hope, indeed to craft a postexilic Judaism. John would work from Jewish themes and communities to interpret the specific sense of disappointment and threat felt by many followers of Jesus. Both prophets would adjudicate between destruction by and accommodation to the empire. These empires were cosmopolitan and pluralistic, not unlike the neo-imperialism of postmodernity, as we shall see.

One needs many eyes indeed to survive with integrity in the urban centers of empire or neo-empire. But if that integrity is not to rigidify into a defensive identity formation, one might also need Ezekiel's wondrous vehicle, which flies in the face of despair. Why has John dispensed with the magic chariot? Does the deity no longer motor about? Did "He" get glued to the throne of an unmoving transcendence? In terms of tradition history, John represents the tendency to replace *Hekhalot* with *Merkhava*, or throne-room, mysticism.[29] Yet his Apocalypse has—characteristic of other *Merkhava* narratives (such as

Akhiva)—retained elements of the chariot symbolism. John's multi-eyed creatures thus suggest indeed "the more or less untransformed detritus of the previous system."[30] We do not read the loss of the multidirectional mobility of the chariot and the metastasis of its eyes onto and into the four creatures as good news.

Liberating Apocalypse

The crisis in the early Christian signifying system, registered in Revelation 4 as the fragment or trace of a prior rupture, suggests to me something more than most current interpretive models suggest. They treat the rupture in terms of religious or cultural persecution brought on by resistance to assimilation in the economies of paganism. John of Patmos's hysterical efforts to delegitimate the prophetess of Thyatyta ("Jezebel" in his name-calling) and to lay down clear lines of control and exclusion among communities suggest that the "conflictual dynamics" do not operate only in relation to imperial oppression. John's text offers meager alternatives for female figuration—arrogant whore, suffering mother, virgin bride. Among them the coalescence of the "whore Jezebel," clearly a competitor for leadership among influential Christians, with the "Great Whore," Rome herself, seems especially cagey.

Misogyny mixes—as it has so often, in so many revolutionary communities—with courageous resistance to economic and cultural injustice. So the crises of the early Christian context in relation to empire and internal conflict may well mirror the rupture among relatively like-minded (feminist, anti-imperialist, deconstructive) readers of Apocalypse two millennia later. "Would that you were either cold or hot," complains John to the church at Laodicea. He certainly gets heat from the progressive and revolutionary traditions of readers, unlike the lukewarm temperature of a mainstream Christian embarrassment with his excesses.

On one side, we hear indeed the hot revolutionary discourse of liberation theology, which almost invariably and transnationally recognizes John of Patmos as a compadre in the struggle. For example, both Allan Boesak and Nestor Miguez recognize the political and economic implications of a liberatory reading of Revelation (see chapter 4).

Justo González's *For the Healing of the Nations* explores the parallelism between the colonized world in the first two centuries of the Christian era and the postcolonial circumstances of today in its reading of the Apocalypse. The Roman Empire was characterized by both cultural pluralism and a widening gap between the wealth of the global elites and the poverty of the colonized majority. The analogy to today's economic and military globilization, indeed Empire, is compelling. This progressive apocalyptic hermeneutic stands in intertextual solidarity with the entire western revolutionary tradition.

Anti-Apocalypse

Characteristic of liberation theologians, Miguez, Boesak, González, and even Elisabeth Schüssler Fiorenza[31] do not worry about the violence of the vision itself, apparently justified by the prior violence of empire. Thus they do not criticize the radical misogyny of apocalypse and its heirs. They do not question the spiritual machismo energizing itself from the cunning icon of the Great Whore's titillating demise. Certainly feminist perspectives can smite traditional left politics with an especially distracting case of cross-eyes. Out of a laudable if doctrinaire interest in keeping "the eye on the prize," that is, focusing Christian energy on the single goal of struggle for social justice, it avoids interpretive ambiguity and ambivalence. It does not, for instance, consider the problem that of "colonial mimicry,"[32] the reinscription of the structures of power in the very act of resistance. It does not problematize the mutual mirroring of "whore" and YHWH, both on their thrones. Feminist readings—prone to our own monofocal gaze, of course—constitute only one means of exposing the oppressive patriarchal models operative within the revolutionary vision.

So then on the other side we have those feminists and deconstructivists chilled by the bloody misogynist martyr's cult of apocalyptic lords and warriors. The title of Lee Quinby's feminist analysis of American culture as ridden with apocalyptic masculinity, *Anti-Apocalypse*, well summarizes this position, further elaborated in *Millennial Seductions*. She refers to her work as "skeptical revelations of an American feminist on Patmos." Tina Pippin offers her own conclusions about John's Apocalypse: "What remains is the misogyny and exclusion by a powerful, wrathful deity. In the Apocalypse, the Kingdom of God is the kingdom of perversity."[33]

Also navigating convergent feminist poststructuralist streams, Stephen Moore challenges atonement theology in its relation to apocalypse. Here he takes his cue from feminist theological work on the relationship between child abuse and the image of God as a father who requires the stripping, humiliation, torture, and death of his Son.[34] Moore indeed zooms right in on our visionary creatures, who are singing and worshipping along with twenty-four elders, to reveal that "the heavenly throne room in Revelation as a whole (in which it functions as the principal setting) mirrors the Roman imperial court." The emperor Domitian was constantly surrounded by twenty-four lictors, officials bearing fasces, and Nero by elite young men functioning as "an imperial cheerleading squad."[35]

Unknowingly, such gendered deconstructions follow the lead of the feminist whom feminist poststructuralists love to dismiss as "essentialist"—Mary Daly, who satirically decried the apocalyptic return of the Lord: "This 'Word' is doublespeak . . . preparing the way for a phallotechnic Second Coming. It is the announcement of the ultimate Armageddon, where armies of cloned Jesus Freaks (christian and/or nonchristian) will range themselves against Hags/Crones, attempting the Final Solution to the 'problem' of Female Force."[36] Daly, the most radical feminist apocalypse of anti-apocalypse, messianically declares her own final Armageddon: "The ultimate contest was wrongly described in the Book of Revelation. . . . The author in his vision failed to note the Holy War waged by Wholly Haggard Whores casting off the bonds of whoredom."[37]

While I may have been more swayed than these feminists by the largely nonwhite voices of the liberation tradition, who read Revelation sympathetically, I too cast my lot with John's Jezebel. A rival Christian prophet, she provokes in John a misogynist tantrum: "Beware, I am throwing her on a bed, and those who commit adultery with her I am throwing into great distress, unless they repent. . . . I will strike her children dead" (2:22-23). The poetics of power, of conquest, of swords and iron rods pitted against female bodies, none too subtly symbolized as "earthen pots" (2:26), penetrates the significatory field of the Apocalypse. A feminist ethic surely cannot in the long run re-veil the misogyny of its revelation.[38]

Whether essentialist or anti-essentialist, however, the repudiations of apocalypse tend to ignore the powerful religious, countercultural, and then secular millennialism stimulating progressive social movements, in particular the nineteenth-century women's movement and each stage of its further development.[39] To the extent that such postmodern feminisms do not take seriously the liberation herme-neutic, which can be dismissed as an essentialist knock-off of the Marxist metanarrative, to that extent they do not account for the eco-nomic, ethnic, and coalitional implications of their own indignant anti-apocalypse.

Double-Edged S/Word

Both the liberation neo-apocalypse and the feminist anti-apocalypse remain pure, hotly mimicking the warrior hierarchy of the domina-tion to be resisted or, in the feminist case, coldly mirroring in its anti-apocalypse the dualism of all apocalyptic demonization. Both modes of progressive thought suffer from unacknowledged binary strategies, which endanger the potential for creative new coalitions. The apoca-lypse reinscribes that which it opposes; the anti-apocalyptic stance reinscribes the apocalypse.

Yet any attempts to resist mere liberal lukewarmth, mere postmod-ern relativism, may produce such dualistic emissions as an inevitable by-product. A sense of power that is liable to discursive rearrange-ments rather than final triumph should prepare one to expect as much. As with the Derridian text, so with this kind of power: "One is always 'inside' power, there is no 'escaping' it, there is no absolute outside where it is concerned."[40] At least however we can recognize the dead ends of such willful or inadvertent apocalyptic politics; we might learn to recognize our ejaculations of unambiguous purity as the leakage of our own uncertainties. We can at least open a few more of our own eyes.

On the particular theological rim (*eschaton*, endtime) where I perch, I need as a feminist both an honest sense of my own precedents in the Christian tradition and a working coalition with those ethnic groups and liberation movements who will for the foreseeable future (which has already extended much further than John could foresee or could have tolerated) find their plight mirrored in John's radical anti-imperialism. One risks on this boundary being spit out as lukewarm, though actually the temperature feels more variant, subject to chills and fevers.[41] This has led me to inhabit what I call *counter-apocalypse*:

a critical edge—perhaps the two-edged tongue after all—that shares much of anti-apocalyptic critique. But it acknowledges the debt of all radical political traditions to that very apocalypse. Therefore it recognizes the counter-apocalypse as itself a form of apocalypse: I hope one of disclosure rather than final closure.

Apocalypse without Vision?

But then it turns out that Derrida had come already. I would not mention the peculiar sensation of post-apocalypse, of an unveiling of that which had been veiled precisely in its prior apocalypse—a post-apocalyptic (cha)grin—had I not suspected that my "I" here mirrors something of the postmillennial moment. Now, having written my way through to the counter-apocalypse, wanting to be done—"it is finished"—with the texts and topics of the End, I reread Derrida's "Of an Apocalyptic Tone" and find the pivotal insight of my counter-apocalypse folded into his "apocalyptic *pli* [fold, envelope, letter, habit, message]."[42] I do not gaze at all these winking eyes alone. A cloud, indeed a crowd, of witnesses—prominent among them those who have built their reputation on the shifting sands of the ever-receding endtimes—shares the varieties and intensities of post-apocalyptic perturbation. Some time in the last millennium I had read the following sentence as closure:

> Now here, precisely, is announced—as promise or threat—an apocalypse without apocalypse, an apocalypse without vision, without truth, without revelation, envois (for the "come" is plural in itself, in oneself), addresses without message and without destination, without sender or decidable addressee, without last judgment, without any other eschatology than the tone of the "Come," its very differance, an apocalypse beyond good and evil.[43]

Worst of both worlds, I had thought: granting the status of a transcendent "beyond" to its own demystification, we are left with a facile Nietzsche, finality without discovery, "without" with no remainder, "Come" with no content—the empty gesture without the zen of emptiness. I had perhaps held out not for this erasure of vision, truth, disclosure, message, destination—but rather for the proliferation of visions and truths that becomes possible when the "last" is subtracted from the judgment, when the single, the One, the Only, the Final is taken away from the truth—leaving not nothing but a liberating pro-liferation, which after all resonated with other deconstructive tones, with the polytonalities of dissemination and the multiple. And I still hold out. I still see the people perishing without a vision. And I am still trying to tell some truth—all the more so because of negotiating the mendacious reassurances, the sincere (white?) lies to which even the most progressive theology is always tempted, the confusion of faith with belief, of metaphor with proposition. Derrida even carica-tures the apocalyptic message—thinking more perhaps of its echo in politics, philosophy, psychoanalysis: "We're alone in the world, I'm the only one able to reveal to you the truth or the destination, I tell you it, I give it to you, come, let us be for a moment, we who don't yet know who we are, a moment before the end the sole survivors, the only ones to stay awake, it will be so much better."[44] Not truth but its monotone, its "monotonotheism,"[45] poses as the "only one." So in the name of the multitonality of truths and the multiplication of visions, I confess to my unveiling (after the fact, after the book) within that same almost anti-apocalyptic essay the key to counter-apocalypse: "Everything that can now inspire a de-mystifying desire regarding the apocalyptic tone, namely a desire for light, for lucid vigilance, for the elucidating vigil, for truth— . . . it is already a citation or a recitation of John."[46]

Ah, then he mirrors in John the very impulse with which we might deconstruct the apocalypse itself: "You have tested those who claim to be apostles but are not, and have found them to be false" (2:2). Bringing to light the circularity of the enlightened critics of all the false apocalypses—among whom must ipso facto belong true anti-apocalypticists—Derrida asks the question from which there may be no exit: "Shall we thus continue in the best apocalyptic tradition to denounce false apocalypses?"[47] In other words, the denunciation of the apocalypse always mirrors the apocalypse. Derrida makes clear the political risk of his own denunciation: "Nothing is less conserva-tive than the apocalyptic genre." It is not a matter of reaching some more enlightened, more progressive vantage point—some saturation of eyes—from which to unmask the conservatism of the apocalyptic ends. Now Derrida folds the question into itself, asking it in its famous form: "Since the habit [pli] has already been acquired, I am not going to multiply the examples; the end approaches, but the apocalypse is long-lived. The question remains and comes back: what can be the limits of a demystification?"[48] By asking this question, Derrida steps off the track of an apocalypticism all the more relentless for its ability to mask itself as deconstruction—as the ultimate, the final strategy of unmasking. Yet he precisely does not step outside of the text of Revelation. "And what if this outside of apocalypse were *inside* the apocalypse?"[49] Rather, he lets it yield up its own opening. He cites its last chapter, in his preferred translation: "Do not seal up the words of the inspiration of this volume." He remains faithful to the radical interiority of the work of deconstruction—prey to itself. It took my own long and clumsy struggle within the radicalisms of the apocalyptic tradition to hear, to see the grace of that double opening. It does not seem like much, perhaps. Perhaps as a theologian, denizen of an archaic discipline, one is grateful for a mere crumb from the Parisian table. I think rather that our own eucharistic banquet loses its taste without some analogue to the Derridian predation.

The Postmodern Bible reads, via Mark C. Taylor, the Derridian "apocalypse without apocalypse" as "an/apocalypse": a felicitous rendition, undeveloped yet almost parallel to the apocalypse retained in counter-apocalypse. For this an/apocalypse, "the text does not reveal but is revealed—as text, writing, scripture."[50] We have already noted Revelation's core imperative: "Write!" Yet we are reading differently here: we are failing to deny the text's capacity to reveal. In this the "counter" remains after all more active, more engaged in an ironic mimicry, than the prefix "an," a simple negation, can support. We are only denying the text's—this text's, any text's—claim to an ultimate or certain truth, for a revelation of the one and only good.

We are allowing the "Come!" some content that Derrida might well want purged. But then he surely recognizes the provenance of all purges. John Caputo has read this "*Viens*" (come) in a fresh "tone": the apocalypse that the apocalypse is without, comes into its own. "For inasmuch as apocalypticism is the call of this 'come,' a hymn and recitative of *viens*, then deconstruction is apocalyptic through and through, *grâce à Dieu* [by the grace of God], and Derrida would never think of shedding his apocalyptic tone."[51] Moreover, Caputo reads in this tone Derrida's debt to the messianism of Walter Benjamin, as well as to the alterity of Levinas, both translated into Derrida's own "Jewishness without Judaism":

Viens, oui, oui, [English: Come, yes, yes] is an upbeat and affirmative tone of passionate affirmation, maybe even a slightly Jewish tone, by which we open ourselves to the event and shift into messianic time. The passion of Derrida's apocalyptic tone is not dire fire and brimstone, not a wild-eyed declamation of imminent doom, nor is he trying to terrorize his critics with a forecast of eternal damnation. . . . The apocalyptic tone recently adapted in deconstruction is upbeat and affirmative, expectant and hopeful, positively dreamy, dreaming of the impossible.[52]

Caputo returns fervently to the convergence of John's final "Come!" with Derrida's *Viens:* "Can John keep his Apocalypse absolutely safe and sealed tight from deconstruction? . . . What could 'seal' John's message off? There, *là*, is the opening for which Derrida, on cat-soft paws, was searching. The Lord told John expressly not to seal it off (Rev. 22:10), to keep it open!"[53] Thus Derrida is a cat prowling among the stranger apocalyptic creatures, finding the crack, keeping it open.

For if apocalypse, which translates as "unveiling," "disclosure," stays open, then the threat of omnicidal closure may begin to dissipate into the crack. In the face of the bitter closures of John's unequaled dualisms of the good and the evil, of now and then, old and new, we and they, keeping it open seems almost enough. It spares us the apocalyptic reruns of pro and con. It gives respite from the habit of renewal through revenge. But of course undecidability remains a necessary but not sufficient cause of any renewal worth singing about.

Not that the opening now should be (again) reinscribed as a mere means to some End—as of full gender/sex/race/culture equality and *differance.* But in order for the very process of opening to sustain itself, there may need to be some content, some commitment, some decision to open. A hermeneutic of uncertainty is not identical to a theory of undecidability: we decide in favor of the multiple and in favor of some pluralities more than others. Theology need not now return to fill the deconstructive void, to plug the opening, and in effect to close it up again. Rather, it has been operating (if somewhat between the lines, as befits a modest witness) all along, pleading, praying, winking, hosting a polyperspectival view—apocalypse not without vision but without one vision; dis/closure of the multivision.

Apoca/Lips

As for the apocalyptic *Viens*, it will keep coming. Even Luce Iriga-ray, no later than Derrida, was waiting for what is to "come." There in the early 1980s she also and just as startlingly, just as irreducibly, had recourse to the apocalypse: "Waiting for parousia would require keeping all one's senses alert. Not destroyed, not covered, not 'dirt-ied,' our senses would be open."[54] Without her we might not find the *body* of deconstruction. Why does it take a woman to recall us to our senses? This lost body is not female only, but it is nobody without the female. The opening of the senses requires more than the opening of a text—even as her text opens into the senses. But here virtually alone among poststructuralist Parisians, she invokes pneumatology, the study of spirit and spiritual things: "Keeping the senses alert means being attentive in flesh and in spirit." That is most intensively a theological proposition, no mere opening, but the opening by and in which I unveil myself as woman, by which my senses and even perhaps, again, my eyes open. To wit: "If God and the other are to be unveiled," she writes then, full throttle apocalyptic, "I too must unveil myself (I should not expect God to do this for me. Not this time. . .)."[55] Her star-tling allusion to Joachim of Fiore and his third epoch, "the third era of the West might, at last, be the era of the couple: of the spirit and the bride," is evidence of her turning like Derrida to the end of the book of the end of the Book (Rev. 20:17). The great feminist prophet of the "lips," the body parable of a subjectivity that is "neither one nor two" but multiple, has unexpectedly unveiled an apoca/liptic orifice for French feminism. Not shortchanging the Joachite heritage, she states apodictically: "The spirit and the bride invite beyond geneaological destiny to the era of the wedding and the festival of the world. To the time of a theology of the breath in its horizontal and vertical becom-ing, with no murders."[56]

This is no coy literary device. Irigaray has joined the choir of feminist theologians.[57] She seeks not an apophatic nothingness, but a sensuous incarnation of God as female. The aim would be unlimited incarna-tion, not the single incarnation of a son, not even the dyadic one of a couple, but of all that is "drawn into the mystery of a word that seeks its incarnation."[58] I pray that her pneumatology of the couple, because it chooses the gender-ambiguous Spirit rather than the couple actu-ally celebrated in John's pericope, the Lamb and the New Jerusalem,

Certainly it sidesteps the slaughterhouse atonement. Still, here too we
need to keep our eyes open. Apocalyptic invocation always runs the
risk of the binaries, of the absolute purity of a purged future, from
which we will always need an opening—a gap, an apophasis. Before it
comes to murder. Before it comes.

Kissing God's Body

What comes, matters. It materializes. It makes a *differance*. Wounded
and wondrous, reading and read, animal/vegetable/mineral/mechan-
ical/divine, the eyes see kaleidoscopically, seeing perhaps Irigaray's
infini, the unfinished? A counter-apocalypse reveals that revelation is
not *one*, not that it is *not*. Derrida proposed the "fiction" of a single
apocalyptic tone, "that *the* apocalyptic tone is not the effect of a gener-
alized derailment, of a *Verstimmung* multiplying the voices and making
the tones shift, opening each word to the haunting memory of the
other in an unmasterable polytonality."[59] We might now reverse the
fiction, invite the derailment, and welcome the multiplicative polytonality. This untoward quartet of creatures is noisy, they see and sing.
Their harmonies might shriek dissonantly to our hearing, yet they do
sing *together*. A theologian at least can invoke the carnival of creatures,
the festival of the world.

The carnivalesque delight of our scene—despite John's general
grimness—suggests itself in the midrash of the *Hekhalot Rabbati*, which
describes how the *Chayyot* sport with YHWH in his heavenly throne
room, kissing and caressing him, flapping their wings ecstatically, playing music and dancing about (13:4). Then we are told: "They reveal
their faces (to Him), but the King of Glory hides His face, lest the
expanses of heaven burst before the King of Beauty, Splendor, Loveli-
ness, Comeliness, Fairness, Radiance, Attractiveness, Brilliance."[60]

Long before the stunning scales and photos of the currently observ-
able universe, the beauty (*yofi*) of the "body of God," which it was the
special privilege of the *Hekhalot* mystics to perceive in sensory ecstasy,
had so far manifested itself through cosmic luminaries.[61] Some recent
theologies, such as process theology and the ecotheology of Sallie
McFague, have developed a metaphor of the universe as the "body
of God." If we keep the metaphor light enough for fiction, weighty

enough to matter, then—invoking the poetic license for constructive theology—the creatures' polyopticon might suggest a certain playful panentheism. Most commentators would not agree to the tradition of reading the eyes as a displacement of the divine omniscience.[62] However, the creatures as immediately surrounding the throne do embody through their particular forms the holiness of the inner sanctum. Perhaps as word-free animals, dangerously inaudible to Christians and postmodernists, they incarnate nonetheless the sacred sentience of all creatures. If divine awareness disseminates through their irreducible *differance*, their eyes belong neither properly to themselves nor to God. Eyes, stars, gems twinkle in a Morse code illegible within logocentric eschatology, signaling a future in which we humanoids sing along, just third of four.

PART THREE

FROM END TO BEGINNING

Constructing a
Political Theology
of Love

6

Everywhere and Nowhere: Postcolonial Positions

Columnist and legal theorist Patricia Williams once reported a joke that had been circulating by email: "A grandmother overhears her five-year-old granddaughter playing 'wedding.' The wedding vows go like this: 'You have the right to remain silent. Anything you say may be held against you. You have the right to have an attorney present. You may kiss the bride.'"[1]

Williams comments that this joke shows how much the concept of the police state, for her represented by the Patriot Act, has infiltrated our thinking. What comes to mind for me is the state of the New Creation. Its ritual is the wedding of the Warrior Lamb with the Bride, the utopian New Jerusalem who descends from above—only to be deployed as legitimation of future totalitarianisms. A United States police state would not resemble a utopian totalitarianism but instead undergo the more ambiguous and insidious process that Derrida calls "the totalitarianization of democracy." It begins with a mass willingness to give up democratic rights for the sake of security. Call in the cops and the cowboys! Send them overseas! The four horsemen wave their guns and gallop.

This global cowboy occupies the space that the French sociologist Zygmunt Bauman has designated as the "global frontierland." In the age of transnational corporations and transnational terrorists, the boundaries of the modern nation-state begin to yield to a new boundlessness. The terrorists, he notes, are "everywhere and nowhere," and they are mimicked by a military empire that can attack anywhere it pleases. Both freely violate national sovereignties.[2] As the first European colonizers approached inhabited space as dark, empty, and available for colonization, so the current neocolonizers treat a far more densely inhabited space as underdeveloped, exploitable, and lacking in differential, fully human socio-ecologies.

The modern nation-state was from its foundations imperial, funded by colonization. If modern nation-states are distinguished by their boundaries, *pre*modern and *post*modern empires penetrate boundaries in the interest of infinite self-expansion. In its catastrophic force of deterritorialization, empire provokes apocalypse, the desperate hope for justice imposed from above, reterritorializing the world as the New Heaven and Earth. So the liberating warrior mirrors the conqueror. In the boundless frontier mythology of the United States, the white-hatted good-guy cowboy, going global, fuses strangely with the ancient, globe-trotting, white-horsed Messiah.

No, no, you might insist. What could the sharp-tongued Messiah, wielding the double-edged s/word, have to do, for instance, with a tongue-tied wannabe Caesar from Texas? Or, for that matter, the anti-imperialism of the liberating Lamb with the history of U.S. imperialism? When it comes to an apocalyptic figure for the American, or any, planetary superpower, shouldn't I be thinking of the Beast and the Whore—not the Lamb and the Bride?

No doubt. The doubling and dividing, the mutual mimicry, of these iconic couples—of the Beast-Whore and the Warrior-Bride—calls for a certain theological edginess, a double edge of hermeneutical ambivalence. This dynamism of doubling confuses the dyads of oppressor-oppressed and so sends theology to postcolonial theory for help. Postcolonial theory, a literary species of postcolonialism, refers to a complex set of textual strategies that this chapter can only introduce. While postcolonialism has already made quite an impact upon biblical studies, it has only begun (with important exceptions such as Kwok Pui Lan and Marcella Althaus-Reid) to register upon the discipline of theology.[3] Postcolonial theory does not imply that the world has moved beyond the use of power for global projects of colonization—only beyond the modern colonial form, in which both imperial center and revolutionary periphery were empowered by national identities. Postcolonial theory does not lack its own blind spots; we will

But it will lend theology a sense of the complex and hybrid relations between colonizer and colonized that belie the simple oppositionalisms of either side and that point the way in a neocolonial context toward new, less dyadic, and more coalitional relations—among races, sexes, genders, cultures, and religions.

To strengthen Christian resistance to our own penchant for final solutions means to free the messianic from the imperial imaginary, divine and human. And ultimately it means to claim the fuller messianic hope, the hope that is the genius of biblical eschatology itself, for a justice in love with *this* creation.

Postcolonialism, Liberation Theology, and the Bible

Early Christianity serves as both a matrix and a parable for the colonizing and decolonizing processes of *late* Christianity. If we can assume that Christianity is not too late, nearly two millennia too late, to recover its Jewish sense of justice and its gospel sense of love, it will for the foreseeable future continue to struggle against its own collusion with the whole range of Euro-American colonialism and neocolonialisms. And in this struggle the postcolonial theory associated with scholars such as Franz Fanon, Edward Said, Homi Bhabha, and Gayatri Spivak may be a helpful resource if and only if we do not mistake postcolonialism for some triumphal declaration that colonialism is over and hybridity is hip. Postcolonial theorists have usually focused on the literature of a past colonial regime rather than on the current neocolonialism, or on what Michael Hardt and Antonio Negri famously announced—before and beyond 9/11—to be the postmodern empire.[4] Postcolonial theory is a living and limited movement, claiming no self-sufficient political vision. Robert Young credibly defends postcolonialism against the charges of a certain depoliticizing relativism, by defining it as always a species of anti-imperialism.[5] Moreover, as Gayatri Spivak's internal or auto-critique of postcolonial reason and the "triumphant metropolitan hybrid" demonstrates, postcolonial theory has itself been evolving with(in) the empire.[6] It cannot be superceded by an orthodox left progressivism as merely historicist or literary. But of course the major postcolonial theorists, while dependent on poststructuralist philosophy (particularly Derrida for Young and Spivak, Jacques Lacan and Michel Foucault for Bhabha), are in fact teachers of literature who offer historical readings of colonial and anti-colonial texts. Thus in terms of method they work in greater proximity to the literary-historical hermeneutics of biblical scholars than to theology.

A creative minority of Hebrew and Christian scripture scholars have been critically engaging postcolonial theorists, testing this fresh approach for its relevance to their own context: Fernando Segovia, R. S. Sugirtharajah, Stephen Moore, and Musa Dube have "pioneered" this exploration.[7] This is in part because analysis of early Christian texts quickly unearths the context of the Greco-Roman Empire. For decades liberation-oriented analysis has drawn lessons for present struggles for justice from the striking textual traces of Hebrew, Jewish, and early Christian resistance to oppression. Yet for some reason liberation theology has not stimulated encounters with postcolonial theory within theology proper in the way that it has within biblical hermeneutics. One reason is that systematic theology has been better able than the historicist disciplines to abstract itself from its own originative imperial context.

Indeed the very methods by which theology abstracts from its history are derived from its distinctively *post*biblical history, that is, from its syncretism with the great systems of philosophical abstraction emanating from Hellenism. It is this hybridization of pagan philosophy with biblical metaphor that produced Christian theology as such and so provided the terms of its orthodoxy. These philosophical discourses, themselves rich and various, were carried into the orbit of biblical thought by the engine of Greco-Roman empire. In other words, theology learned from the *metaphysics* of the empire how to abstract from the *politics* of empire. So by positing the ahistorical propositions of Christian orthodoxy as its eternally true foundation, theology has less readily recognized its own complicity in the multiple layers of western colonialism.

Liberation theology, with the irreducible legitimacy of struggle, cracked the hard surface of timeless orthodoxy. Its vision of a new Jerusalem of "clear water free for all"—a society ordered according to principles of economic justice and human dignity—depends for its realization upon the emergence of "the new subject in history." So it shook deeply "from below" the foundations of a church hierarchy claiming its authority "from above." Yet in order to guarantee a final eschatological triumph for the poor, it left largely unquestioned dogmas of divine transcendence and omnipotence. Its God seems to remain, despite the "below" of the poor, the almighty Subject who will deliver (in the future, if not from above) upon the promise of the New Creation. In this it has leaned heavily upon the masculinist metaphors of the lordly *creatio ex nihilo* and the messianic warrior-liberator. As Ivone Gebara, herself working within the context and commitments of Latin American liberation Catholicism, puts it, "the fundamentally anthropocentric and androcentric character of liberation theology appears unquestionable. It speaks of God in human history, a God who in the end remains the Creator and Lord."[8]

Liberation theology tends to content itself with a return to prophetic and apocalyptic anti-imperialism. Since these dimensions of scripture had been so long numbed and suppressed by the established church, such an irruption of liberation motifs was the most potent possible Christian response to the police states of Latin America, South Africa, South Korea, and the inner cities of the United States in the 1970s and 80s. But the liberation hermeneutic pretends—partly of course for purposes of rhetorical strategy, of church pedagogy—that the Bible itself presents an unambiguously liberatory vision. It ignores the acquiescence in classism, xenophobia, authoritarianism, sexism, heterosexism, and violence that burdens much of the canonical text, indeed much of the exodus and prophetic tradition. It does not notice how frequently the apocalyptic Lord of lords and King of kings, bringing on his white horse the empire of God, has inspired the sacred violence of Christian empire.

These are familiar and not antagonistic criticisms. They belong to the long-developing complication and multiplication of the prophetic voice itself, the voice of its auto-critique. Indeed, if, say, a Euro-American feminist voice would not only challenge but ignore or dismiss the liberation tradition, we rightly suspect racism and classism. And, similarly, if a liberation voice silences or ignores that of a native tradition, we register Christian chauvinism, racism, classism. But of course these dismissals have happened routinely. One "new subject history" in practice competes with other emergent "new subjects in history" and is tempted by the messianic *gravitas* of the struggle to shut the other voice out. For example, feminism is seen as a western imperialist threat to race or class solidarity, or vice versa. Such internal struggles are inevitable in a complex self-organizing process. But the question is whether a contextual theology will reinforce the exclusivisms of solidarity or, to the contrary, deconstruct the exclusions for the sake of a wider solidarity.

Is it not precisely the apocalyptic impulse among these voices—especially, perhaps, as they operate within the North American academy—that tended to sharpen an all-or-nothing, unilateral politics of identity? The "poor," the "woman," the "Black," the "lesbian," the "gay," the "Minjung"—each new subject has had its (justly) messianic moment. But then, perhaps inevitably, each has been to a greater or lesser degree reified as a subject matter of theology, its boundaries hardening around an essential core of hermeneutically privileged identity defined in opposition. The proliferation of oppositional identities, each disclosing a new and indispensable demand for justice—what Henry Louis Gates called "the multiplication of the margins"—has had the effect of not only multiplying but dividing progressive coalitions within and beyond Christianity. Have these ethical oppositionalisms not fallen all too autonomically into the pattern of religious exclusivism, at first apocalyptic in its absolutes, then supersessionist in its orthodoxy? We have had too much experience in the church and the academy of, for instance, a hermeneutical violence among women, within and across ethnicities: the nonconstructive criticisms, the willful misreadings, the righteous indignation that confuses professional ego with prophetic courage. Nonetheless, these various voices of liberation do express the spirit at its apocalyptic edge, ever ready to spit the other out as lukewarm, compromised, in bed with the enemy—even as adulteress and whore.

The Difference of Postcolonial Theory

If postcolonial theory is exercising an attractive power among students of theology, students of multiple religious and social contexts, this seems to me to emanate from a charged "between," a complex space, a space between the bounded contexts, between the uncompromising identities and positionalities. Does such a between-space suggest compromise or rather an honest interdependence? How would it relate to the everywhere-nowhere space of fluid postmodern boundaries, a space of mass economic migration and of transnational capitalism, of terror and of empire?

In Homi Bhabha's thinking, postcoloniality as a discourse of resistance requires an "interstitial perspective."[9] In the interstices our split differences braid ambiguously together. And therein may lie also, he suggests (if rather faintly), the possibility of new and more resilient global coalitions, in which our variously impure and hybrid identities can morph from political liability into asset. This is crucial for those of us who have never been able fully to release our creative force because we feel somehow tainted, misfitting, unconvinced, mixed, mixed up. Such an interstitial perspective seems to offer a space in which we can risk new politico-religious experimentations. Here ethical discernment as to what is better and what is worse frees itself from the habit of apocalypse, the habit of good versus evil. It can cure itself first of all from the fallacy of the binary alternative that allows it to perceive no alternative to the either/or of absolute truth (good!) versus mere relativism (evil!).

In truth, between the binary poles lie not just grey shadows but the whole spectrum of flaming colors. Here *justice* can be—with prophetic passion—liberated from the phantasmagoria of *judgment*. But then by the same token there is a test I find crucial to the use of postcolonial theory: Does postcolonial theory work to supercede liberation theology? Inasmuch as it does, I suspect it is working precisely as one fears, to relativize any revolutionary impulse, to dissipate the political energy of transformation, to replace active movements of change with clever postures of transgression. Like the poststructuralist theory it draws from, postcoloniality would tend then toward the oxymoronic stance of an absolute relativism. But within theology so far, postcoloniality functions not as a supersession but instead as a supplement to the liberation tradition. In the deconstructive sense of supplementarity, it offers an internal challenge to the certainties and dichotomies that tempt every emancipatory discourse to render final judgment rather than justice. Thus Chela Sandoval warns against the political identity analogues to the Stalin effect as "the revolutionary form of frozen meta-ideologizing." In other words, revolutionary-left ideology can become orthodoxy and push toward a totalitarian effect. The point of thawing out the frozen oppositional identities is not to depoliticize but, as I read this fresh Latina voice, to allow a new political energy to flow. "The unhinging of consciousness from its political commitment to the differential mode permits any oppositional practice to become only another version of dominant ideology, another version of supremacism."[10] This "differential mode"—refusing to reduce particularity to totality, to unity—would prevent the reifying of *my* difference, *our* difference, as supreme.

Writing in a related theoretical vein, Rey Chow as a Chinese American feminist questions the paradigm of "ethnicity" so crucial to the politics of difference. She draws a surprising analogy to Max Weber's analysis of the Protestant ethic. She observes the way a particular leftist narrative structure places "the victim in the (modernist) position of a captive, whose salvation lies in resistance and protest, activities that are aimed at ending exploitation (and boundaries) and bringing about universal justice." Is she treading here on progressive religious toes? "For Weber," she writes, "precisely this narrative of resistance and protest, this moral preoccupation with universal justice, is what constitutes the efficacy of the capitalist spirit." Thus she quips: "I protest, therefore I am." Rey Chow's book title is itself a great pun: *The Protestant Eth*n*ic and the Spirit of Capitalism.*[11]

The question of the piety of protest does not stop with the trajectory of the Protestant Reformation. In the present context—textual and political—we cannot fail to recognize the sources of a spiritualized resistance movement in the apocalyptic tradition (which was both deployed and constrained by the Reformers). It protests, if not modern capitalism and imperialism, certainly the global empire of its time, with its trade in luxury goods, cash crops, and human lives.[12] A postcolonial theology cannot disavow our dependence on this biblical tradition of protest. But it may help us to outgrow the pious prevarications of progressive theopolitics. The policing of our positionalities, the postures of purity—the meta-ideologizing—have made coalition politics too difficult, just when it is most needed.

Cowboys and Crusaders

Why are planetary coalitions so needful now? Because globalization in its predatory forms will not be countered locally. It requires a global response. It requires something like what such varying thinkers as Bauman, Derrida, Spivak, and David Held call the new cosmopolitanism, a democratic cosmopolitanism. Such global coalitions as the still promising and undefined anti-globalization movement, with related NGOs (nongovernmental organizations), may figure more significantly than the United Nations. Progressive interfaith religious support is already endemic to these coalitions, and it can be dramatically strengthened as we claim our counter-apocalyptic confidence. The process of globalization in its neocolonialist economic form now uses the apocalyptic terrorist as endless pretext for global military hegemony and preemption—and thus for an empire garbed in the messianic whiteness of Christiamerican rightness. Nor is the self-contradicting hybrid of apocalyptic anti-imperial Messiah and imperial Beast new, but in the old habit of Christian empire, this monster Messiah of the single superpower now rides postmodern technology (see chapter 3). And since the end of the Cold War, this superpower is no longer, as Richard Falk explains, deterred.[13] Once restrained by the Soviet Union, it no longer needs to compete with socialism, to make nice to labor and minorities at home or to the poor and the majorities abroad. It is another kind of virtue, of have-a-nice-day innocence, blandly brutal, lending a cowboy style to a medieval tradition.

That would be the tradition of the Crusades, which lured the Bush dynasty irresistibly eastward. Christians now can stand back, as virtually no one at the time seems to have done, and declare the Crusades an ungodly mutation of revelation into annihilation. I have argued that we will be more effective in resisting the crusading pattern if we do not pretend that either the Bible or Christian interpreters stand free and pure of a certain holy brutality. Neither the neo-apocalypse characteristic of most liberation thought nor the anti-apocalypse characteristic of most feminist and critical theory will in this resistance serve us as well as a constructive counter-apocalypse—itself a strategy of the interstices, neither enclosed within the walls of a privileged salvation nor assailing the walls from outside. It holds open the fluid passage between inside and out, us and them, the familiar and the foreign. Thus it finds revelation—sometimes tinged with apocalyptic anxiety, sometimes expressed in loving revelry—in the diverse codes and languages through which we may craft postcolonial interrelations.

The Crusades preceded the modern colonialisms that stimulated twentieth-century postcolonialisms. But just a year after the 1099 "liberation" of Jerusalem, with its slaughter of the Muslim population, we read of a bizarrely *pre*-postcolonial moment. Fulcher of Chartres wrote of the western colonists settled in the new Crusader states of the Middle East: "We have become Orientals. The Italian and the Frenchmen of yesterday have been transplanted and become men of Galilee and Palestine. . . . We have already forgotten the land of our birth; who now remembers it?" He tells how men have taken to wife Syrian or Armenian women, sometimes even a baptized Saracen. "We use various languages. . . . The native as well as the colonist has become polyglot and trust brings the most widely separated races together. . . . The colonist has now become almost a native and the immigrant is one with the inhabitants."[14] Perhaps this romantic view of a harmonious new ethnic, cultural, and linguistic hybridity aimed to attract more European settlers. In the meantime the Crusader states maintained constant aggression toward the Muslims, if mitigated by a post-apocalyptic pragmatism.

What is startling, however, is that this kind of polyglot hybridity, this exchange of a western for an "oriental" identity, could even serve as an ideal image, that it could even count as romantic and function as propaganda. It unhinges any simplistic account of the opposition of Eurocentric aggression to its invaded aliens. It also belies facile celebrations of hybridity or polyglossia. Fulcher thus offers a premodern illustration of the postcolonial analysis of hybridity as an effect of colonization. Bhabha insists that the ensuing interdependence produces an ambivalent desire for the other who has become part of the self—a desire felt, but felt very differently, by both the colonizer and the colonized. In this premodern Christian discourse of polyglossia and trust, of racial reconciliation and immigrant identity, we can find no legitimation for any crusade. We can however note that images of foreign women and of mixed marriage signal the work of desire in this oddly literal, stunningly hybrid New Jerusalem. It is a desire to appropriate, to unify. Yet desire itself, as Emmanuel Lévinas explains, resists the imperial project. It partakes of the infinite and so hints at that which infinitely exceeds any appropriation. The interplay of desire and polyglossia renders these characters not merely reprehensible but also somehow recognizable, across the divide of a thousand years.

So the apocalyptic crusade holds the Christian west together in opposition to Islam across a millennium—even as it splits the difference. And the difference refracts dizzyingly. The apocalypse has not lost its grip on western history, a history that cycles menacingly back around its eastern origin, its Jerusalem, ideologizing and meta-ideologizing. The history of the effects of early Christianity can and will be read to denounce conquest and occupation as well as to legitimate it. From one point of view we gallop into the land of the other like the Lord of lords. From the other's point of view we look like the all-consuming Beast, the Whore-Queen with whom the client elites and *comprador* classes of the world are in bed. From the point of view of a counter-apocalypse, the United States confuses itself with the messianic Lord and thus fuses with the imperial Whore.

Whores of Apocalypse

But as soon as I yield to this tempting invective, I lose my distance from John of Patmos: in the interest of an anti-imperial gesture I defile my own and every other woman's sex. The ancient compulsion to brand the masculine enemy as a promiscuous female feeds its symbolism from the sexual denigration of actual women.[15] The misogynist iconography of the Book of Revelation is unlike anything in the Gospels. Their Jesus does not define his inner circle as "virgins," those "who had not defiled themselves with women" (Rev. 14:4), nor display any venom toward the gender or sexuality of women. But it is not just the religious extremisms among the three families of Abraham that manufacture the venom. It appears among the icons of postcolonial theory as well.

Thus Rey Chow analyzes Franz Fanon's acrimonious, lengthy denigrations of the females of his own ethnic group. He is dealing with the no doubt bottomless perplexities of sex, race, and internalized racism when he lambastes women for supposedly repeating to themselves this mantra: "whiten the race, save the race." But his language is extraordinarily violent here: "It is always essential," he mocks, "to avoid falling back into the pit of niggerhood, and every woman in the Antilles, whether in a casual flirtation or in a serious affair, is determined to select the least black of the men." Rey Chow asks this: "In thus literally marking the women as whores and converting them into traitors to their own community, could Fanon be seen as being caught in a familiar condition, the condition of *ressentiment*?" Chow, herself implicated in postcolonial theory, otherwise admires Fanon's achievement. But here she examines cases of a wide phenomenon of interethnic "ressentiment," in which sex plays a vivid role. This ressentiment tends, she writes, "to assume its hold fiercely on the postcolonized ethnic community." As in Fanon's work, the effect is directed in no uncertain terms against the women of the community, "who are at once pathologized for their sexual lewdness and repudiated for having sold out to white supremacy."[16]

African American womanist theologians such as Delores Williams, Kelly Brown Douglas, and Karen Baker-Fletcher have long tracked such double-jeopardies within the work of racial solidarity. Sexism crosses every class, racial, and religious line and unfortunately sometimes intensifies among culturally humiliated men. Given the presumed analogies of the contexts of marginalization and colonization today with the positionality of the Book of Revelation, Chow's analysis illumines a disturbing symptom of prophetic protest. From ancient times, the rage against the empire and those who compromise with it was readily displaced onto real or symbolic females. Jezebel and the Great Whore are the prime figures of sleazy, self-serving sellout. So we may not want to imagine that we could purge apocalyptic resentment of its misogyny and neatly redirect it toward a proper postcolonial target such as "capitalism," "globalization," or "imperialism." "Behold I will strike her children dead." Is this collateral damage in the cause of justice?

Just Love

We cannot purify apocalypse. It will only reveal our own impurities. I suggest instead that we absorb these impurities as the very building blocks of a New Jerusalem worth inhabiting. All the shattered hopes, the defiled utopias, the half-cocked imperialisms and avenging terrorisms—their fallout pervades the history from which we must recycle and renew the creation. But if it is not the absolute purity of judgment that will adjudicate among the possibilities, what then? Nothing but relativism, nihilism, mutters the apocalypse . . . I think not. I think it is rather the sacrality of annihilation that produces nihilism. We have seen the difference collapse between the presumed opposites of the apocalyptic absolute and the globalizing relativism, the messianic machismo and the imperial indifference, the Lamb and the Whore.

What third space opens? What path is there within the relationalities that comprise us without neutralizing and devaluing our lives? Is this not where the great resource of early Christianity, yet absent to the apocalypse, comes into play? Is this not the infinite path of desire, the path we call, for lack of a better word, *love*? Alone it solves nothing, it sentimentalizes, it privatizes. Indeed it lends its name to every violence done for love of one's own community, one's own tradition. Saint Bernard, the great mystic of love, almost single-handedly launched the second Crusade, with never a thought as to the possibility of loving the enemy, the Muslim.

I do not know if we—for example, mainstream Christians in the United States, that omnivorous "we" from which I cannot abstract myself—will do better, for all our shades of Christian love-justice. But some of us are attending to the dross and damage of our history. Before its cycling, crusading totalisms we have felt our fear rising. We witness the *left*over progressivism of the twentieth century, the shards of social movement, the incapacity of liberalism to organize a coherent program amid its multiplying margins, the absolute and almost immobile red-blue polarization of the nation. At this moment it is not the purity of any *new* New Jerusalem that moves me, let alone the indignant protests of aging academic radicals. It is invariably some pulse of imperfect love that once again casts out fear. Then my eyes open to signs of hope, the beginnings of new coalitions everywhere, ready not to supercede but to recycle the old social movements.

Thus, for one imperfect instance, I just spent a couple days in the Seoul household of a couple of theologians, indeed, a married couple, former students of mine who have been unable because of their feminist commitments to teach full-time as theologians in their conservative Christian traditions. They teach English to survive. They gave hours daily to the internet campaign that blocked a reactionary impeachment attempt and saw elected the most progressive parliament in South Korean democratic history. They are working through two different explicitly feminist lists, and after the political campaign they have continued to inscribe upon the Web with risky honesty their insights into sexuality, spirituality, ecology, and power. Noteworthy was the postmodernity of this sophisticated electronic campaign, a portent of a new politics of virtual space. But what was *moving* was the undoubtedly loving energy with which these two marginalized theologians nurtured the relationality of this new semiotic Web and of their own maturing partnership. And in this I glimpsed something of a new movement, alive with democratic energies that have been cynically dissipated in my own country.

If we practice the connection of political movement to the capacity to be moved and to move—to give and receive love—what might be possible? The classical Christian God could not receive love or be moved by it. "He" was the Unmoved Mover, transcending any reciprocity. But what might be possible if after all God does not just perform love as a condescending imperial mercy but actually loves, is loved, *is* love?

Among postcolonial theorists, love, as we shall see in the next chapter, is bursting out of the interstices. Sandoval's *Methodology of the Oppressed* proposes the coordination of the oppositional positions that are "democratizing, semiotic, deconstructive of every supremacy" through what she calls "the physics of love." "Love as social movement is enacted by revolutionary, mobile, and global coalitions of citizen-activists who are allied through the apparatus of emancipation."[17] Indeed who could now trust any "apparatus of emancipation" that is not lubricated by love? How could it hold together all our differences?

And there's the rub: we have not learned to hold them together. We have not gotten over our habits of apocalyptic opposition. It is the right wing of religion and of politics that thrives in a homogenizing unity. And the post-Stalinist left cannot compete on the grounds of the absolute. It will always fail if it tries. Its constituency is and will increasingly be compounded of dizzying, self-respecting differences—of ethnicity, sexuality, class, culture, religion, agenda. Unlike the old left and the new right, the "physics of love" will not abide any residues of a police state. As citizen-activists and as citizen-theologians, we repress our own ethical and ethnic hybridities, our sexual and gender complexities, our mixtures of privilege and suffering, at peril to our strength. But the solidarity possible through our multifarious differences entails not *relativism* but *relationalism*. The progressive option in religion and in politics will find its strength in its planetary web of interdependent diversity.

The bad news is: such a cosmopolitan democracy exists nowhere. The good news: the signs of it are planetary. And its flexible, decentered love force may prove more durable, within the shifting spatiality of postmodernity, than the preemptive omnipotence of empire. And as the majority of the human and indeed nonhuman populations of the planet suffer an undisguised, unjustifiable, delegitimated injustice, we will see not only apocalyptic panic but also movements of self-organizing social justice. We won't get gospel love without justice—only a privatizing, clinging, greedy emotion that yields to fear rather than casts it out. And we won't get apocalyptic justice without love, but only the police state of judgment, behind whose indignant purities the Messiah-Bride pair collapses into the copulating Whore-Beast of empire. In answer it is not a harmless churchy balance of love and justice that we need, but an *ekklesia* (community) of just love, an eros that readies us for deadly dangers and for delightful surprises.

In the challenging times ahead, the love that casts out fear will continue to energize each of us, I hope, to coalesce with each other, to try fresh experiments and old disciplines of coalition not because we are sure we are right, but perhaps because together, almost too late, we begin to realize a far-fetched desire. If desire partakes of the infinite *in* the finite, it may be the only way to counter the boundless greed of empire *for* the finite. If our postcolonial ambivalence does not dissolve into the postmodernity of everywhere and the utopia of nowhere, it will get us—somewhere.

The divinity of everywhere is only incarnate *somewhere*. Nowhere is it not incarnate *somehow*. The physics of that love moves us like the sun and other stars, like a strange attractor, luring this indeterminate chaosmos toward the unknown. As this counter-apocalypse sets no date for (the next version of) The End, we might as well begin again. We go to meet the future—the ultimate blind date. We look toward the hope of a festive justice that can sustain us all. Fortunately, the original meaning of *apokaluptein*—to unveil the bride—takes on queer new meanings these days.

You may now kiss the bride.

7

The Love Supplement: Christianity and Empire

Empire requires that all relations be accidental.
—Michael Hardt and Antonio Negri,
Empire

We are talking about using the strongest mobilizing discourse in the world in a certain way, for the globe, not merely for Fourth World uplift. . . . This learning can only be attempted through the supplementation of collective effort by love.
—Gayatri Chakravorty Spivak,
A Critique of Postcolonial Reason

Christian theology suffers from an imperial condition. Shall we start there, with that proposition, but as a *theological* proposition? Then it is not a denunciation lobbed from some indignant outside but also not another hand-wringing confession or liberal hair shirt of Christianity itself. No, this proposition is first of all descriptive. Empire indicates an organizational illness of history, deadly but not necessarily terminal. "Imperial society is always and everywhere breaking down," write Hardt and Negri of empire's state of "corruption." "But this does not mean that it is necessarily heading to ruin."[1] Let us say that empire is a recurrent condition, an extraordinarily adaptive one that grows rapidly in each new manifestation, voraciously consuming the space it occupies. It mixes together otherwise separated cultures, ramming populations into relations extrinsic to their indigenous integrities, "accidental" in the classical sense intended by Hardt and Negri—violating their own "necessity," their "essential" identities. Yet within imperial space, allergy may also turn into attraction; alien traditions may collude and mingle, birthing all manner of strange religio-cultural hybrid.

Christianity is the greatest of these. When it opened its young mouth to speak, it spoke in the many tongues of empire—nations and languages colonized by Rome, and before that Greece, and before that Babylon, which had first dispersed the Jews into imperial space. That diaspora was positioned throughout the cities of empire, and its representatives circulated continuously back along Roman roads to Jerusalem. Yet even these visitors were aliens to each other, divided and conquered by difference. So the linguistic miracle of that day, the Pentecost of polyglossia, stunned the disciples (women and men, young and old, gentile and Jew) into mission. They believed, rapturously, with no naiveté as to the risk, that they could communicate beyond every boundary, that the community could keep its many selves in tune, and still stay in motion. A global gambit: that love might not get lost in translation.

They were not wrong. It might not. But as we know, in the interest of translation, the language, the logos, of Hellenism provided *theologos* itself. "Theology," a Platonic concept, effected the syncretism of a colonized Judaism with a colonizing Hellenism. Christian arguments—and increasingly faith was about arguments rather than witness—were persuasive inasmuch as they absorbed the imperial metaphysics. The ontology of changeless, dispassionate Being, of eternal essence presiding over the "accidents" of space, time, and becoming, came to preside over the church itself. Relationships among beings are conceived as "accidental"; that is, relationships do not affect the "essence" or identity of a being.

How could love survive this metaphysics? What is love when its relations are unilateral, accidental to the One who loves? How is it different from power? Still, this metaphysical shift did not in itself make the church an instrument of the empire. The church until Constantine could resist the idolatry of the empire, of its gods of power, wealth, and conquest, in part *because* it could argue in its philosophical terms, not only witness in its tongues. But the hermeneutical cost of absorbing the metaphysics of the empire was high.

With its imperial success, the church, one might argue, absorbed an *idolatry of identity*: a metaphysical Babel of unity, an identity that homogenized the multiplicities it absorbed, that either excluded or subordinated every creaturely other, alter, subaltern. God was cast in the image of this ontological identity, infused with a power that could only be—lacking all receptivity and reciprocity—all-controlling. Thus the Jewish Creator-Judge of history was hybridized with the unmoved Mover; and soon the sovereign Father of orthodoxy—"God of power and might," as many of our liturgies still chant—manfully merged with the sovereignty of the state. He spoke in the one tongue of Rome. The "globalatinization" (Derrida) project overtook the originative polyglossia. We need not rehash here the ensuing history of conquests, unifications, crusades, expulsions, of new, more modern conquests for Christ, commerce, and king, and of the "anglobalization" of the earth.[2] But whether colonized or colonizing, Christianity has not existed in abstraction from empire.

There is no pre-colonial Christianity. But—as the last chapter began to ask—is there a postcolonial Christianity? If so, the postcolonial contribution properly comes from the peripheries, diasporas, and boundary zones of empire, from people in some sense speaking for those peoples who over the past century and a half achieved national independence and yet now find themselves subject to new forms of imperial subjugation. From Latin America, the Caribbean, Asia, Africa, Oceania, where formally a postcolonial situation obtains, come the new voices of Christianity, of a self-renewing Christianity continuing the polyglossia (not infrequently literally Pentecostal and accompanied by glossolalia, speech not of many languages but exceeding language itself). And as all those continents have cast their people back into the urban centers of the west, postcolonial theology will take place in the strange spatiality of the postmodern globe, both "here" and "there"—"ours" and "theirs."

Still, it remains unclear whether someone like me (privileged as Euro-American, natively Anglophone, tenured feminist, etc.) can write "postcolonial theology" (any more than, earlier, liberation theology). Amid the perforated boundaries and unrealized hopes this theology both examines and risks, it is also unclear why *not*. If progressive, contextual theology is not simply imagined to be the expression of a pure identity and its politics, then it is important that defectors from imperial presumption embrace the postcolonial hope. I can at the very least, and for the sake of constructive Christian theology itself, consider the postcolonial potential of theology—and the theological potential of postcolonial theory.

Constructive theology refers to the broad endeavor to situate spiritual discourse within an irreducible sense of context. In this endeavor I find postcolonialism indispensable in grasping the overlaps, flows, and constitutive relations *within* and *between* contexts. But these contexts, precisely by way of their "interstitial perspectives," map onto a global space that is *not only postcolonial but transnational.* That transnational globalization lends itself to a new manifestation of empire. What has yet to be determined is whether postcolonial theory helps us to discern our current global condition, whether the *interstitial* will help to confront the *imperial.* There are multiple critical readings of "empire" available to theological discourse, and some of the most cogent are wary of postcolonial theory. Here I consider in depth two such critiques, that of the foundationally secular political analysis of Michael Hardt and Antonio Negri (whose work I have discussed briefly in earlier chapters) and that of the foundationally Christian theology of John Milbank, all socialists of immense vision and all allergic to postcolonial theory. I will also consider in detail the auto-critique of postcolonial theory set forth in Gayatri Spivak's *Critique of Postcolonial Reason* (also mentioned in earlier chapters), precisely as it impinges on the theological edge of the "global."

Here's what I want to suggest: only to the extent that postcolonial theory helps to map the spatiotemporality of the current globalization can it orient theologians in our *constructive* (that is, not only biblical-historical-critical) project. For the work of theology has been global from the start—inevitably, because of its imperial condition. But much more: this Christian globalism also and from the start translates into a *counter-imperial ecology of love.* The global quality of the Christian perspective would therefore give it the capacity and the obligation to confront the imperial globalism—from within, to be sure, but from an inside not enclosed but porous in space and time, carved out and complicated by its own diasporas and margins, embedded in a nonhuman and now also colonized nature. By entering into certain current debates on religion, empire, and the postcolonial as a way of contextualizing Christianity within the present global order, we may

Mutually Assured Vulnerability

Let us reconsider the spatiality of the present global order. When the
sociologist Zygmunt Bauman (with a bit of apocalyptic hyperbole)
proclaimed ours "*the era of the end of space*," he meant in fact the end of
a particular kind of bounded, national spatiality, "the annihilation of
the protective capacity of space." This end is a "double-edged sword," he
continues (intending no allusion to the double-edged Word of John's
Apocalypse). It exposes "the new condition of the *mutually assured vulnerability* of all politically separated parts of the globe." The endless new
"war on terrorism" presumes a new extraterritorial sense of space. It
is effected, he suggests, by a kind of mimetic violence between the terrorist and the state. Both, he suggests, undermine "the constraints on
their freedom to ignore or push aside the 'laws of countries' wherever
such laws feel inconvenient for the purpose at hand."[3] This extraterritorial "(un)space," with its flexible, unbounded, and unwinnable war,
its "floating coalitions,"[4] comprises a new frontier-land. Bauman names
the older space of bounded state territories "modern," suggesting the
postmodernity of the new boundary-transgressive global (un)space.
Reminiscent of David Harvey's characterization of "the condition of
postmodernity" as the "annihilation of space through time" by way of
the instantaneous transmission of capital and information, as well as
new patterns of travel and migration, this collapse of the boundaries
of modern spatiotemporality yields a postmodern "space of flows." Yet
it tends toward homogeneity, not toward the emphatic difference and
pluralism of postmodern theory.

   "The sacrosanct division between inside and outside, that charted
the realm of existential security and set the itinerary for future transcendence, has been all but obliterated." There is *no outside* any more,
continues Bauman. "We are all 'in,' with nothing left outside."[5] The
theological allusion is not casual. What would such a loss of transcendence, of a space and a time beyond this world, signify? Historically,
the boundary separating the "inside"—as the church triumphant,
New Jerusalem, or City of God—from the outside of the irredeemable
world transferred to the boundary of the Christian empire and thence

to the secular modern states the very sacredness of their "sacrosanct division."[6] Nothing left outside: this might entail simple atheism and the collapse of meaning along with the space of transcendence. Or it might mean that the divine can no longer be situated in a standard theistic beyond and therefore that it cannot offer the false sense of security encoded in the classical construct of the changeless transcendence, with its omnipotence that could unilaterally intervene to reward, punish, or rescue. So is there a possibility that a more radically relational theology can rise to the postmodern occasion? Within this spatiality of mutually assured vulnerability, might the human species choose to honor that mutual—and universal—vulnerability? For Bauman, "the bluff of local solutions to planetary problems" has been called. He calls for a new cosmopolitanism, which takes up again "the keen search for common humanity," in which an "ethic of hospitality"[7] is a tautology—in which "ethics is hospitality."[8] If this common vulnerability can be reduced neither to its biological basis nor to an imperial dream, might its practice not require an alternative theology? Might it summon the spiritual cosmopolitanism initiated in the ancient imperative of hospitality to the alien and the immigrant? Might it invite all local contexts—within its so problematically shared *cosmos*—to nest within its branches?

Empire of the Third Millennium

Bauman does not mention the influential text by Hardt and Negri that had boldly named this space of the global flows of "money, technology, people, and goods": "Empire is materializing before our very eyes" in postmodernity, the modern nation-state has less and less power to regulate these flows. "The decline in sovereignty of nation-states, however, does not mean that sovereignty as such has declined."[9] Hardt and Negri read "Empire" precisely not in terms of the imperialism of the European states but as "a *decentered* and *deterritorializing* apparatus of rule that progressively incorporates the entire global realm within its open, expanding frontiers." Note, however, how eerily their analysis echoes the hybridity of postcolonial theory: "Empire manages hybrid identities, flexible hierarchies, and plural exchanges through modulating networks of command. The distinct national colors of the imperialist map of the world have merged and blended in the imperial global rainbow."[10] The authors trace a movement from modern to imperial sovereignty as "from dialectical opposition to the management of hybridities, from the place of modern sovereignty to the nonplace of Empire, from crisis to corruption."[11]

Hardt and Negri read globalization as "economic postmodernization." What then of the production of theoretical knowledge in the forms often clumped within the "postmodern"—specifically postcolonialism and the kindred discourse of poststructuralism? They diagnose both—with sympathy—as "symptoms of the passage to empire."[12] They read the postmodern fixation upon the influence of the Enlightenment as the source of domination, and the postcolonialist battle with the remnants of the accompanying European colonialism as failing to recognize the new form of domination that looms over us today. "What if the dominating powers that are the intended object of critique have mutated in such a way as to departmentalize any such postmodernist challenge? In short, what if a new paradigm of power, a *postmodern sovereignty*, has come to replace the modern paradigm and rule through differential hierarchies of the hybrid and fragmentary subjectivities that these theorists celebrate?"[13] This is a question that any postcolonial theology must answer. I think it can. For the supersessionism implied in their question collapses in the course of their own argument.

Hardt and Negri charge that "those who advocate a politics of difference, fluidity, and hybridity in order to challenge the binaries and essentialism of modern sovereignty have been outflanked by the strategies of power."[14] For "empire is not a weak echo of modern imperialisms but a fundamentally new form of rule."[15] If power—as we see it manifest in transnational corporate capitalism—now deploys difference and hybridity, these postmodern and postcolonial theorists, charge Hardt and Negri, are "pushing against an open door."[16] Defining *empire* as corruption and, indeed, as "impure or hybrid," Hardt and Negri seem to imagine a future purity, indeed ontological necessity, of revolt. Postcolonial theory, by contrast, examines the binaries of modernity precisely as delusions of purity, often nationalist and often revolutionary. But contrary to the standard criticisms, postcolonial theory does not "celebrate" hybridity. Homi Bhabha, its most famous theorist, reads hybridity as the product of colonization, as the largely involuntary internalization of oppression by the oppressed. But he then argues "against the purists of difference" for a productive ambivalence derived from that very hybridity.[17] For the hybridity, with its well-managed "mimic-men," can morph into the unmanageable, into a parody of its managers.

Yet the question persists: just how "subversive" is the parody? Is it really much more than a stylized mimicry of older European forms of domination? Hardt and Negri take Bhabha on directly: "We should be careful to recognize the form of the dominating power that serves as the enemy (and really the negative foundation) in this postcolonialist framework. Power is assumed to operate exclusively through a dialectical and binary structure. The only form of domination Bhabha recognizes, in other words, is that of modern sovereignty."[18] In their view, postcolonial theory is beating a dead horse. Their critique is helpful, but only to the degree that binary power and its rigidity of boundaries have actually been liquidated by the fluidity of the postmodern market.

Soon after *Empire* was published, the world was subjected to a new U.S. manifestation of state sovereignty, aggressively *nationalist* and boundary-fixated, yet *also* (as Bauman has noted) transgressive of modern understandings of space, law, and boundary. So now what sense of "empire" is most helpful?[19] Is it the global economics that triumphantly transgresses the boundaries of modern nation-states in its late-capitalist "free trade" fluidity? Or is it the nationalism of the American Empire, exercising an unprecedented military power and preemptive "right" over the globe? Are these identical projects, or rather, allied but finally incompatible modes of hegemony? The door of empire both opens and shuts. It apparently swings on a well-greased hinge.

At any rate we can hardly assume as Hardt and Negri seem to that rigid boundaries are a thing of the past (and postcolonial theory therefore only helpful in reading history). For instance, more people died at the Mexican-American border in the five years prior to 9/11 than during the whole history of the Berlin Wall.[20] One must recognize the *flexible* capacity of global economics to impose *rigid boundaries* as needed. Indeed this is precisely what Hardt and Negri do acknowledge when they analyze "imperial racist theory" as a "theory of segregation"—that is, of boundaries—rather than of organic hierarchy, as no less "essentialist" than the older biological racism in establishing "social separation and segregation." So it would seem that within postmodern empire there are after all "rigid limits to the flexibility and compatibility of cultures."[21] In other words, their Empire—in both economistic and military form—reinscribes the modern binaries at its convenience. Their supersessionist and linear model of time collapses in this reinscription.

If, moreover, the new resistance "means first of all struggling within and constructing against Empire, on its hybrid, modulating terrains,"[22] then it would seem after all that postcolonial theories of the hybrid help us to map such terrain. Notions of "subversive mimicry," "strategic essentialism," and the deconstruction of power/knowledge (for example, "Orientalism") and Edward Said's "contrapuntal" rather than merely oppositional strategy—in short the theoretical apparatus of postcolonialism—do operate "within" this imperial condition. But who doesn't? Hardt and Negri cite a major critic of postcolonial theory, Gyan Prakash, who charges that "the postcolonial exists as an aftermath, as an after—after being worked over by colonialism." "This," they comment, "may make postcolonialist theory a very productive tool for rereading history, but it is entirely insufficient for theorizing contemporary global power."[23] But isn't the "imperial condition" a present tense that reproduces the past structure of power, indeed, a condition in which, in Bhabha's words, "the 'past present' becomes part of the necessity, not the nostalgia, of living"?[24]

I am not at any rate arguing for the "sufficiency" of postcolonial (or any) theory, only for its value. Indeed it is as *historical* analysis that postcolonialism has lent itself to the biblical-historical disciplines. Theology by contrast takes—from that very history—an *eschatological* orientation: toward the future as currently emergent. But if sufficiency *were* the criterion, certainly the transmutation of "empire" after 9/11 into a neonationalist expansionism demonstrates the limits of Hardt and Negri's own model. The "open door" of empire shuts in their face. *Empire*'s dismissal of postcolonial theories as "symptoms of passage" is finally disingenuous. For Hardt and Negri's own work—"struggling within and constructing against Empire"—is no less symptomatic than any other postmodern text. They too locate their project *within* the "hybrid terrain" of the postmodern imperial condition. But their hope is stronger, more straightforwardly revolutionary than Bhabha's. As they read Marx, modern capitalism enabled better resistance to oppression than did feudalism; so "this new imperial terrain provides greater possibilities for creation and liberation."[25]

If these encouraging possibilities remain vague, the authors offer praise to its new spirit: it "makes resistance into counterpower and makes rebellion into a project of love." It should perhaps not surprise theological readers to find ourselves confronted—at the tail end of a fully secular-socialist text—with a sudden epiphany of love. When a barely possible hope must be summoned, eschatology becomes irresistible. In "the irrepressible lightness and joy of being communist," they propose a single model: none other than Saint Francis. His "joyous life," predicated on voluntary poverty, "including all of being and nature, the animals, sister moon, brother sun," offers an "innocent" revolution, one "no power will control."

One feels disarmed by such lightness and joy—of being theological. This last-minute turn to Christianity—*amor ex machina*—would benefit from some actual engagement of the love mysticisms. It might lose its innocence and gain in credibility. In its passion for a justice that draws delight from the full life and space of the creation, we recognize gestures not only of a long tradition of Christian communism, in which the revolutionary energy of Europe was apocalyptically coded, but of the momentous contemporary tradition of ecotheology. We are left with the theopolitical hint—a hint not to be shunned, but rather developed by way of a postcolonial theology Hardt and Negri reject both as theology and as postcolonial theory—of a Spirit materially embracing all that is.

No Love Lost

Suitably, *empire* has found its way into theology—indeed in the same essay in which occurs a rare theological discussion of postcolonial theory. John Milbank, proponent of a "'gothic vision' in its socialist, Christian, variant,"[26] offered a strong response to the 9/11 attacks, one that holds up several years later. He read the "unprecedented outrage" following the attacks as the sign of a U.S. "crisis of sovereignty."[27] For a non-state entity to assault a state with a warlike gesture "threatens the very idea of the State." Thus the "hidden glee in the official outrage" suggests that certain factions found a chance to "reinscribe State sovereignty." They could now engage in a continuous war "to ensure that free market exchange processes are not exploited by the enemies of capitalism." Milbank invokes Hardt and Negri's account of the "American neo-Roman imperialism," as it "includes" the Other by subordinating it "to unremitting uniformity." He contrasts this present empire with the older, European imperialism, "which held the other at a subordinated distance, permitting its otherness, even while subordinating it for the sake of an exploitation of natural and human resources."[28]

Milbank is satisfied that "Hardt and Negri concede that neo-empire outdoes old empire in vileness."[29] He thereby seems to miss *Empire*'s central point. Hardt and Negri claimed that a new sovereignty is precisely not *reinscribing* but *replacing* that of the nation-state. Moreover, they do not see the new empire as necessarily worse than former projects of domination. Rather, they warn against any nostalgia for the bounded nation-state. They believe that the very globalization that has insidiously collapsed space into commodifiable information will yield its own forms of resistance. Milbank, however, straightforwardly avows the superiority of the British Empire, which included "many utopian imperialist schemes that went even beyond this subordination, and tended to deploy the peripheries and 'savage' to mock the center and 'civilized.'"

Might Milbank be mirroring postcolonial theory's analysis of the parodic mimicry of colonizer and colonized? By no means! "Such nuances are shockingly overlooked in *pseudo-left-wing American 'postcolonial' discourses*, which actually assist the ideology of the American Right by implying the original 'innocence' of the United States as a once colonized nation and its natural solidarity with all the colonized."[30] This is, rather "shockingly," quite a misreading. "Natural solidarity" belongs to the discourse of essential identities that postcolonial theory exists to contest. And there is no work of postcolonial theory that resembles his caricature of "American" postcolonialism, by which he means presumably such immigrant intellectuals as Said, Bhabha, and Spivak. Robert Young, in his historical study, does consider "the more complicated situation of the USA, which was both settler colony and imperial power." But he implies no innocence there.[31] According to Milbank these implications of "original innocence" (certainly nowhere explicated) "tend to conceal the fact that American . neo-colonialism is far more insidious than the older variety. It does not attend to cultural difference (like, for example, the British law code for India)."[32] Indeed the American Empire, through a virtual Wild West of diplomatic vulgarity, cultural homogenization, and maximum firepower, pursues a more voracious—and more truly *global*—

dominance than any before. And certainly postcolonial theory was generated in a literary-historical focus on the aftermath of European colonialism. But Milbank, a white British theologian, is without any noticeable sense of irony framing nonwhite, British-educated postcolonial theorists as "pseudo-radical" (unlike the truly "radical orthodoxy") because they fail to appreciate the British Empire's sensitivity to difference.

Nonetheless, Milbank's call to "abandon our global idolatrous worship of secularized absolute sovereignty and its empty pursuit of power, in West and East alike,"[33] belongs among the prophetic discourses of Jewish, Christian, and Muslim social justice. indeed Milbank argues for a return to "*the biblical and Platonic-Aristotelian metaphysical legacy common to Christianity, Judaism and Islam.*" This "common vision" would "trust that human wisdom can imitate, imperfectly but truly, something of an eternal order of justice."[34] Yet such a vision of a single changeless order, a timeless origin that humanity should harmoniously imitate, represents precisely the wrong basis for justice, at least according to all postcolonialist or postmodern theories of difference. These challenge the Eurocentric and all too historical mold of just this "eternal order." The "common vision" of radical orthodoxy, unlike the cosmopolitanism of Bauman or even Hardt and Negri, thus takes largely the negative form of polemics against poststructuralism.[35]

Has Milbank, who is only interested in those elements of Islam derived from the (Platonic-Aristotelian) west, replaced a gross and present paradigm of homogenization with an older one—indeed with the *original,* the very metaphysics of *origin*? In the midst of a historic "crisis of sovereignty" he offers the most ahistorical of solutions: the metaphysics of an eternal order, from which human justice must be derived by a hierarchy of "imitation." This platonic mimesis provides the very "original" that deconstruction deconstructs—a deconstruction politicized by postcolonial theory.[36] Bhabha reads the political effect of this legacy of the western "origin" in the colonized "mimic men," who as "not quite, not white" remain a shadowy facsimile of the European "original."[37] They are measured—and measure themselves—against European standards. Yet it is this classical legacy whose passing Milbank laments when he elsewhere articulates "gothic space." The gothic would cure "the fascist tendency of all non-socialist corporatist thought." It is a "complex space," antidote to the homogeneity of late-capitalist space, which in its present unilateralist form

is indeed raising the question of fascism.[38] He distinguishes it also
from papal ecclesiology, the "space" of a "sublimely confident autho-
rization."[39] But he just as firmly separates gothic space from another
catholicism, that of liberation theology, which he reduces to a kind
of *time*, a "fusion of teleological historicism with a mystical activism
which fetishizes outcomes."[40] The "fetish" would presumably refer
to the eschatological hope for history—distant to be sure from the
Platonic eternity! Unfortunately, this "complex space" is too simple
to accommodate a respectful engagement of liberation movements,
let alone their postcolonial variants, nor, on the other hand, does it
move toward a needed *ecological* challenge to the liberation focus on
(human) history at the expense of (nonhuman) nature.[41]

Yet Milbank does invoke a certain ecology of divine love. He gives
little positive meaning to the complex space, beyond the hint of the
"doubly exceeding body of Christ, the Other Space of our history."[42]
It is, however, another beautiful hint. Again, we are left—where
political hope turns vague—with bodily Love. If theology "wishes to
think again God's love, and think creation as the manifestation of
that love"—as surely we do—"then it must entirely evacuate philosophy, which is metaphysics."[43] By "philosophy" here he does not count,
for instance, the late Plato (upon whose theory of participation and
"extra-cosmic logos" he depends). He means any theory not baptized
by that orthodox, creedal Christianity authorized, it so happens, by
the Roman Empire. Like many postliberal theologians, he would have
his postmodern *anti*-metaphysics and eat the cake of classical metaphysics, too.[44] No wonder this orthodox anti-modernism maintains a
tone of polemical competition with postcolonial and poststructuralist theories. The latter postmodernists challenge the Eurocentrism
of modernity, while the former wish to deepen that center's claim.
Indeed Milbank laments the lost authority of the universalizing order
(the order of essence and accident) that grew up—gothically—amidst
the ruins of Rome.

Ironies abound. The imperial apologists of *Foreign Affairs* also
claim a gothic vision: "In the twenty-first century, characterized like
the European Middle Ages by a universal (if problematic) high culture with a universal language, the U.S. military plays an extraordinary and inimitable role. It has become, whether Americans or others
like it or not, the ultimate guarantor of international order."[45] This
political order is abhorrent to Milbank—and any other progressive

Christian. And yet the anglobalization of the world inaugurated by the British Empire is being completed by the American Empire. The current project of domination is theoretically justified by the conglomerate of a certain Christianity with the explicitly classical, universalist political philosophy of the neoconservatives affiliated with the New American Century, the think tank that lobbied for the Iraq war long before 9/11.[46] In the face of a "world at risk of cascading disorder," "order" is thus guaranteed[47] (an order that Jon Stewart, comedian and host of cable television's *The Daily Show*, headlines as the "*Mess-o'-potamia*"). Such order stakes its universal claim not on love but on power. It makes itself the original, the essential, the indispensable—which other systems are then to imitate.

As to the gothic, I share with Milbank a certain awe before the sheltering mystery of those cathedrals. Is it possible to revisit their complex spatiality—and their humanized, suffering Christ—without a return to the verticalism of the vision, its timeless Truth sending Crusades eastward in space; without a return to *any* of the unquestionable orders of the west, superimposed upon the rest?

We have read two influential, socialist denunciations of the present imperium, one a communism of pure immanence, the other a theology of classical transcendence. Both in the end invoke a medieval Christian sanctity of love. Both appeal to the space of the creation. Both tap deep Christian dreams of a new order. I am trying to honor the shared dream. It is for that reason that I have interrogated their respective dismissals of postcolonial theory. Different but parallel purisms lie behind the dismissal of a theory that deconstructs every claim to purity, however progressive. It will help us to avoid the crypto-imperialism of an exclusionary Truth and the cryptotheology of revolutionary innocence. We turn thus to a key postcolonial thinker—and yet another incongruous epiphany of love amid the ruins and renewals of empire.

The Love Supplement

Gayatri Chakravorty Spivak writes, "Indeed, it is my conviction that the internationality of ecological justice in that impossible, undivided world of which one must dream, in view of the impossibility for which one must work, obsessively, cannot be reached by invoking any of the so-called great religions of the world because the history of their greatness is too deeply imbricated in the narrative of the ebb and flow of power."[48] She has kept postcolonial theory in mind of gender and economics, as they transverse the racialized representations of the subaltern. Suddenly, in this passage, she breaks into ecological discourse. Spivak's "impossible, undivided world" borrows—by way of a long critical engagement—the sense of "the impossible" from Jacques Derrida.[49] It means for neither of them a literal impossibility. It belongs amid his tropes of the "messianic," the "promise," the "come!" These biblically charged signifiers do not signal the coming of a literal or national messiah but the political space of the "democracy to come" (a democracy not yet seen) and of a quite eschatological "indeconstructibility of justice."[50] If I mark the distance between "the promise" and the present as the "improbable" rather than the impossible, it is only to make (appear) more *possible* the work and the world for which Spivak calls.

Spivak positions her "dream"—in its eschatological improbability—in precisely the space this essay has been exploring. In its internationalism it shares Bhabha's insistence upon the "inter" space, the interstices of nations, cultures, and their ambivalent subjects. And she reinforces the postcolonial critique of the self-avowedly "great world religions," the patriarchies that expanded *greatly* with the energy of empire. But unlike other postcolonialists, she begins to map her internationality onto the nonhuman earth. As the religions of the west subdued "nature" (along with woman and other "others") she makes common cause with the "global movement for non-Eurocentric ecological justice."[51] And with the ecology of this gesture, a new gesture of and in postcolonialism, she addresses the link between the *interstitial* and the *global*. This terrestrial globalism occurs toward the conclusion of her ambitious work, *A Critique of Postcolonial Reason*. Mimicking Kant's *Critique of Pure Reason*—the great internal check to western rationality—she tests postcolonial theory from within. It has never claimed purity nor confused the reasonable with the western. But she calls to task both the "triumphalist self-declared hybrid" (who in dropping any Marxist economic analysis colludes with capitalist globalization) and the leftist academic (who in a delusion of direct action misses the Eurocentrism of Marx).[52] But it is, intriguingly, the supplementing of economic analysis with ecological analysis that effects her own shift.

> Upon the body of this North/South world, and to maintain the
> fantastic cartography of the World Bank map, yet another kind of
> unification is being practiced. . . . What we have to notice here is
> that the developing national states are not only linked by the com-
> mon thread of profound ecological loss, the loss of forest and river
> as foundation of life, but also plagued by the complicity, however
> apparently remote, of the power lines of local developers with the
> forces of global capital.[53]

Mapping this global *oikos* (Greek for "house"; root of *eco*logy, *eco*n-
omy)—comprised of the interaction of economic and ecological
forces—she rebukes "the glib theorists of globality-talk," neo-liberal
advocates of globalization. But she also targets "those who still whinge
on about old-style imperialism" (modern Marxists and, I presume,
postcolonial theorists not yet hip to the new transnationalism of
Empire). Sounding suddenly like an ecofeminist, she articulates the
bodily connections of justice, gender, and the global ecology. In subsequent writing she will "propose the planet to overwrite the globe."
Stretching beyond the abstractable, commodifiable "globe," indeed
beyond where other poststructuralists and postcolonialists have dared
or even desired to go, she announces that "today it is planetarity that
we are called to imagine."[54] But I will stay within her *Critique* to follow
the genesis of this fertile idea.

To further her point, she deconstructs a work of a first-world
feminist Marxist who had herself deconstructed the "essentialism"
of a Bangladeshi feminist activist. That Bangladeshi had referred to
women's reproductive capacity as "a natural power we carry within
ourselves."[55] The challenge to a familiar feminist anti-essentialism
(the suspicion of every generalization about nature or femininity)
exhibits Spivak's famous "strategic essentialism" at work. Recall that
(her own) poststructuralism is a fundamental critique of essentialism, that is, of the binary of essence and accident, of a core, original
identity and its extrinsic, changing relations. But the formulaic *anti*-
essentialism may silence all sense of connection to our bodies, our
communities, and our earth. And we might add: the anti-essentialism can itself reduce all sense of identity and so all relations to the
inessential, as surely as can an imperial essentialism. Her "history of
the vanishing present"—the book's poetic subtitle—invokes not just
a disappearing set of cultural practices but also the evanescence of

any identity not fixed in an eternal present, an essential presence. To
be evanescent is not to be accidental, however, but precious and grief-
worthy in one's passing.

Spivak now makes another altogether unexpected move: one we
can only call *theological.* "Having seen the *powerful and risky role played*
by Christian liberation theology, some of us have dreamed of *animist libera-*
tion theologies to girdle the perhaps impossible vision of an ecologically
just world."[56] In one extraordinary sentence, she affirms the work of
liberation theology (heretofore ignored by postcolonial theory) even
as she steps (or dreams) off from its Christianity. Before we imagine
Spivak slouching toward theology, however, we read that "*the name of*
theology is alien to this thinking."[57] Almost in the vein of Thomas Aquinas,
she both affirms and negates the language of theology. "Animism"
does not represent an alternative theology, but a sensibility toward
the nonhuman that has left vestiges among subaltern peoples, the
peoples trapped between and beside the self-designated "great world
religions." These traces have lured the "metropolitan migrant" in the
direction of a postcolonial theology.

Why is the "name of theology" *alien* (if, like other aliens, unavoid-
able!) to this animist liberation dream? "Nature," she hints, "is also
super-nature in this [the animist] way of thinking and knowing. . . . For
nature, the sacred other of the human community, is in this thinking
also bound by the structure of ethical responsibility."[58] She seems to
be thinking against the Christian binary of the supernatural Creator,
in whose image the rational, responsible human is created, and the
remainder of creation—nature. With this opposition, classical theology had indeed prepared the way for the modern dichotomy of human
(essential) culture versus amoral (accidental, inessential, expendable)
nature. The animist—altogether *alive*—nature eludes and exceeds
both the fallen Christian nature and the de-animated nature of scientific modernity. Christian orthodoxy predicated this dualism upon
the nonbiblical doctrine of the *creatio ex nihilo.* And the movement of
liberation theology toward a vision of ecological justice—as well as
an appreciation of tribal, indigenous, or "animist" ways—has indeed
been hindered by the privileging of "history" over "nature."

In fact liberation theologians, such as Leonardo Boff and Ivone
Gebara, and Euro-American ecotheologians, such as Rosemary
Ruether, Sallie McFague, Jay McDaniel, and John Cobb, have long
moved close to the proposed "animist liberation theology" and far

from any dichotomy of nature versus supernature. One wonders if theology is "alien" to Spivak because she doesn't read any.[59] These theologies do remain, if self-critically, within "the ebb and flow" of Christian power (which means within their progressive margins of the church, mostly in the ebb). All these varied ecological theists would concur that nature as "sacred other of the human community" is indeed "bound by the structure of ethical responsibility"—not that animals, plants, and rocks can be judged by human norms, but that they participate responsively within the web of the human world.

Moreover, all of these ecologically oriented theologies would assent to her subsequent statement: "No individual transcendence theology, of being just in this world in view of the next, however the next is underplayed, can bring us to this."[60] She seems to believe she has thereby deconstructed liberation theology. But Spivak's perfunctory critique misses the mark. Perhaps most liberation theology did leave the patriarchal anthropomorphism of a transcendent Lord operative. But even where it lacks an ecological or feminist motif, liberation theology did not just "underplay" the stereotyped "individual transcendence theology." It pits the whole force of its new—collective—subject in history *against* it.[61]

Perhaps only theologians worry about nontheological caricatures of "theology." But in a text that contains such blanket claims as "U.S. based feminism cannot recognize theoretical sophistication in the South,"[62] may we not expect its author to recognize theoretical sophistication in the South of religious movements? In other words, I wonder if her "dream" would be more possible if she did not implicitly exclude the subversive histories and potentialities of an immense class of hybrids. These hybrids contain formative syncretisms of "the great religions" with "animism," of the creative, ambivalent mixes that grew and still grow in the cosmopolitan corners and rural margins of empire, where the faith of the colonizer is mingled jauntily with shamanistic, indigenous, tribal, African, and other alternative practices.[63] Nonetheless, the ecotheological tendency of Spivak's thought symptomatizes an "in-between" of great promise: freeing itself from the orthodox forms of socialism and of religion, there is emerging a *planetary spirituality of the interstices*. No locality can be located apart from its interrelations. Close and alien, intimate and systemic, they add up to the global. But the planetary is greater than the sum of global parts. No theory holds a monopoly on its spatiality. Also taking place in this space is a metamorphosis of Christianity, in a form not interested in religious triumph but in "peace, justice and the integrity of creation," in the language of the World Council of Churches. In its passion for the creation—as eco-social commitment—this version of Christianity suggests a planetary motivation, a cosmopolitan spirit that takes a radically ecumenical form and thus, I believe, makes contact with the *inter*-religious (im)possibility Spivak also seems to sense:

> I have no doubt that we must learn to learn from the original practical ecological philosophies of the world. Again, I am not romanticizing, liberation theology does not romanticize every Christian. We are talking about using the strongest mobilizing discourse in the world in a certain way, for the globe, not merely for Fourth World uplift. . . . This learning can only be attempted through *the supplementation of collective effort by love.*[64]

And so love has appeared once again. It is revealing that postcolonial "love" gets articulated in a mimicry of Christian liberation theology, and so in the creation of this new liberation-animist eco-hybrid. But, after all, the desire for a discourse of new international coalitions emanates from the heart of postcolonial theory. Here the fluidity of boundaries cannot be reduced to a neo-imperial globalization. The needed "collective effort" can only arise across and between boundaries—of nations, faiths, groups, genders. Spivak's love-supplement goes further:

> What deserves the name of love is an effort—over which one has no control yet at which one must not strain—which is slow, attentive on both sides—how does one win the attention of the subaltern without coercion or crisis?—mindchanging on both sides. . . . The necessary collective efforts are to change laws, relations of production, systems of education, and health care. But without the mind-changing one-on-one responsible contact, nothing will stick.[65]

"Love is patient . . . does not insist on its own way" (1 Cor. 13:4). Spivak of course is not citing Paul. Yet when she characterizes love as mind-changing, she could be translating the New Testament *metanoia*. Christianity itself is lost on her. It is not what she needs. But perhaps something Christian theology needs for its own work can be *found* in postcolonial translation? In an empire collapsing space into information, earth into colony, and difference into product, where exacerbated impulse-gratification for the few replaces the hope of a sustainable condition for all, "the responsible self" (H. Richard Niebuhr) faces new temptations and obstructions. The "one-on-one" of love must never be scorned for the sake of the collective. Conversely, it becomes increasingly irresponsible to disdain any hope of a common humanity, a global commons, a common creaturely fate. And so a "collective effort." The common humanity—precisely because it lacks a fixed essence—must be created always, again, and never from nothing. We are all already bound up together in our earthly ecology. If all existence is within and beyond its alienations covenantally bound, *religare,* reconnected "by the structure of ethical responsibility," then all bodies *matter.* But this vision requires an almost inhuman surplus of care. When we who share an ancient text and practice of "love" see postcolonial theory—in a key attempt to think beyond its own preoccupation with an older imperial history—leaping into a spiritual discourse of love, both mocking and mimicking theology itself, might we not welcome the initiative?

Postcolonial Incarnality

As Thomas Mann wrote: "The result is perfect clarity in ambiguity, for love cannot be disembodied even in its most sanctified forms, nor is it without sanctity even at its most fleshly. . . . Love is our sympathy with organic life, the touchingly lustful embrace of what is destined to decay."[66] We have seen an ecological spirituality begin—only begin—to reconfigure the spacetime of postmodernity. The divergent texts considered in this chapter have suggested that there would be nothing *theologically* accidental about the emergence of an ecological motif—precisely there where love begins to overflow its politics. Love cannot be disembodied. And bodies disclose—in the interstices of their *essential* and not accidental relatedness to other bodies—our planetary ecology. Once we free theology from a disembodied paternity, once, in other words, it discovers the open-ended creativity in which all creatures partake, it can disclose the widest context of our embodied life. That creaturely width exceeds the scale of any empire, and yet in the history of the west it has been bound and defined by the succession of imperial powers. Nevertheless, Christianity has always addressed a spacetime beyond any particular context. This sense of transcendence has both infused and constrained the idolatrous immensities of imperial space. In other words, this universal vision has lent itself both to empire and to anti-imperialism. It may now call us, in a liberation apocalypse, to "come out of the empire"[67]—the liberation apocalypse. "Come out of her my people."[68] Or it may call us out of less pure, more complex space: to come out of imperialism.

We are in but not of the empire. The "world" as corrupt and polluted imperial space lives parasitically within "the creation."[69] Thus the earth itself is not "*of this world*" but of the creation. Even within Bauman's "era of the closure of [the modern construct of] space," the space of creation does not close into itself. It is not bounded from within, by a pure immanence, or from without, by a supernatural transcendence. Creation takes form within an infinite ecology of relations.

Without locking into any orthodoxy, let us note that within the biblical traditions we may address that infinity of relations as "You." The infinite might become intimate. It might become loveable. It might become Love. And even this "love cannot be disembodied." Thus theologian Ivone Gebara speaks of the divine as our Sacred Body; others have called the universe the Body of God.[70] It is precisely its embodiment that renders love Christian. This incarnation, this *incarnality*, does not transcend the radical immanence of the infinitely expansive postmodern space. We remain "inside" the global condition, but not as within an enclosure of accidental—external—relations. No relation is pure accident or pure determination; every relation co-constitutes its world, for better or for worse. In the interstices of the creation, new connections are continually created.

This mutual creativity offers little security. It creates at the same time our Mutually Assured Vulnerability. If no human agency—personal, economic, military—stands outside of the web of relations, all—and now with a stark techno-global necessity—remain subject to blowback.[71] Human interrelatedness remains as terrible as it is loveable. The complex spatiotemporality of the globe will not lessen the current threat that whatever cannot be appropriated to the imperial monoculture may be annihilated. The tongues of flame dancing upon the heads of our diversity may be extinguished. The empire will strike and be struck back. The love of the Song of Songs, the love that is as strong as death, may not conquer the forces of domination. But it may permit, between us, Mann's "perfect clarity in ambiguity." It may per-

134   mit within us Minh Ha's "accurate tuning of our many selves."[72] In the "interstitial intimacy" of increasingly mingled and mixed existences, ambivalence can be, as Bhabha insists, productive. The tongues still wag, dance, and burn. An ecologically sustainable and ethically hospitable earth remains maddeningly *possible*.

8

The Democracy of Creation: Chaosmos and Counter-Apocalypse

We dream of a tender justice; we yearn for democracy and
respect for the *res publica*.
　　　　　　　　　—Ivone Gebara, *Out of the Depths*

Have you entered into the springs of the sea,
Or walked in the recesses of the deep?
Have the gates of death been revealed to you,
Or have you seen the gates of deep darkness?
Have you comprehended the expanse of the earth?
　　　　　　　　　—Job 38:16-18

Theology always means—whatever else it means—theopolitics. However deeply faith may retreat into privacy, God-talk begins and ends among the *res publica*, the "public things." So when it is mobilized as a power ploy, not only democracy but religion is wounded. For instance, when the first U.S. president of the new millennium was asked if he had ever consulted his father before ordering the invasion of Iraq, he replied that "he is the wrong father to appeal to in terms of strength; there is a higher father that I appeal to."[1] The Son-of-God posture may strike some as piety, others as blasphemy—and others as just embarrassing. But the theopolitical code is unmistakable: this Father God is defined by strength. This is not the love-daddy of Jesus but the omnipotence of the divine warrior. But in this last chapter I do not want to come (again) to the endtime oxymoron of Messiah and Beast. Let us now meditate on the power in beginning.

From End to Beginning

The two may be separated by nothing but a breath. That breath makes all the difference. Might we meditate—even in writing, even in reading—not just upon but *in* that breath? Let us consider a theopolitics in the spirit of that breath, or the breath that is that spirit. For I suspect that you (if I may) finally cannot abide a theopolitics that chokes the spirit, that, however presumably progressive, cultivates a condition of chronic moral indignation. If we reduce the world to ethics or politics, we flatten it. Then we only mirror in reverse the shrunken cosmos achieved by a conservative salvation history. For the complex biblical stories of beginning and ending, creation and apocalypse, have been subordinated to an unbending, orthodox construction, that of a linear order moving from an absolute origin to an absolute closure, like a power-line between two poles. It was from the start a line of power.

My own work has been driven to deconstruct the timeline at its two ends, origin and *telos* (goal). I have found the fallacy of the power-line not only dangerous to the health of the earth but downright unbiblical. Indeed that timeline underlies all the projects of a manly messianism in its global "strength" and all-too-Christian expansiveness. Of course it is tempting to answer the timeline of imperial messianism with a tightly strung opposite, that of a revolutionary messianism, just as galvanizing, reductive, and absolute in its claims. Yet many of us no longer find any warrior apocalypse inspiring. Every form of sharply bounded identity, every absolute of religion or roots or story or tradition or gender or sex or race or ethnicity or class, already appears to us simplistic, brittle, and a bit desperate in its fabrication. These defended identities, these differences—marked as Other, as monster, as enemy or chaos by the warriors of domination—all now demand breathing room. The others, the subalterns, must not be suffocated in their own alterity. In this very otherness they want to open their pores—even to each other. We all deserve a discourse and a practice expressive of our complexity, our dimensionality. The discourse of mere difference, some of us (perhaps influenced by postcolonial theory or process theology) might claim, has proved inadequate. The theology I labor to articulate, the theology of becoming, represents one sort of transitional alternative beyond mere alterity, an alternative in becoming, in *genesis.*

In order to make our differences in the world we had best breathe into the interstices of our differences—the between spaces, where our dimensions fold in and out of each other, in and out of God. After all, the world is made of the cosmic dimensionality that Genesis calls "heaven and earth." We may read the world itself as *genesis,* a great poem of becoming. Let us then seek clues for our *theopolitics*—for the way change is initiated, the way a beginning is made—in the *theopoetics* of creation.

The Chaos of Creation

According to the mathematical theory of chaos, minute changes can have immense effects. Scientists formulate this principle of complex dynamical systems (such as weather) as "extreme sensitivity to initial conditions." Popularized as the butterfly effect, "extreme sensitivity" means that through the subtle iterations and interconnections of wind currents, landscapes, and temperatures and the resulting amplifications, the flap of a butterfly's wing in New Jersey can cause an avalanche in the Himalayas. This is a secret lesson in hermeneutics. If we read a numbingly familiar text (like the opening of Genesis) just a bit differently, the entire system can shift. And the second verse of the Bible is all about a complex chaotic system: "And the earth was *tohuvabohu* and darkness was on the face of *tehom* and *ruach elohim* was vibrating over the face of the waters." Might this theory of initial conditions have something to tell us about all our beginnings, our chaos, and our complexity? Translate *tohuvabohu* as "without form and wild." *Bohu* hardly exists as a word on its own; it is added to *tohu* to intensify, to iterate, to rhyme. Indeed its reason *is* its rhyme. *Tehom* means "deep," "ocean," and "chaos." And it was Hermann Gunkel a century ago, followed by Gerhard von Rad, who first translated the rhythmic, oscillating motion of Spirit (*mrphet*) as "vibrate." Even these translational minutiae have theopoetic significance![2]

Science cannot dictate terms to faith. But Christian theology has always and necessarily developed its cosmologies from nonbiblical paradigms (the church fathers took from Plato, Aquinas from Aristotle). We just don't want to get stuck in assumptions about the universe that are passé and predictable. So we draw not scientific objectivity but a metaphoric clue from the postmodern sciences of chaos and complexity—sciences of nonlinear systems.

The clue is to a mystery: the mystery *of the missing chaos*. Historically, verse two of Genesis had virtually disappeared (in plain sight!) from theology by the fourth century. When it began to reappear about a hundred years ago, it did so, as we shall see, in strangely hostile ways. Why does it matter now? The creation stories of Genesis continue to materialize disproportionately immense theopolitical effects. It is not that Genesis gives a pseudoscientific account of the origin of things but that it poetically channels that "extreme sensitivity to initial conditions"—and remains susceptible to radically divergent readings.

How did its chaos get lost? In a nutshell: it got swept under the carpet of the doctrine of *creatio ex nihilo*. Theologians keep declaring that this creation by the Word from absolute nothing is the evident meaning of the Bible. Yet there is *no such biblical teaching*: not in Genesis, not elsewhere.[3] Of course the *ex nihilo* dogma solved a hermeneutical problem: if there is something already there when God creates, does this not constrain divine omnipotence? Ironically, it was Basilides, a Christian Gnostic, who seems to have first invented the full doctrine of creation from absolutely nothing: he couldn't imagine the transcendent Godhead having anything to do with chaotic materiality. Irenaeus, writing against the Gnostics, then made the *ex nihilo* a touchstone of *orthodox* Christianity: he could deal with God touching matter but not with a God less powerful than his opponents. For the emergent orthodoxy, the *ex nihilo* doctrine became an argument for God's omnipotence because any pre-existing stuff or energy would somehow constrain divine power. Some recognized the problem: Hermogenes wrote against both the Gnostic and the ecclesial *ex nihilo*, recognizing that it anchored in an immoral notion of power, an omnipotence to which was sacrificed divine goodness. So he was also declared a heretic. Most theologians soon learned just to skip verse 2. Augustine, however, creatively struggled with it. He even argued for "multiple true interpretations." Yet his solution, that the chaos is the first stage of creation, seemed to many theologians just as problematic. The twentieth-century theologian Karl Barth, rejecting the Augustinian solution and also recognizing the biblical challenge to the *ex nihilo*, called the verse a "veritable *crux interpretum*." How can God create chaos, if the work of creating is nothing other than the work of ordering, of commanding and separating? Chaos for him *is* the nothingness that God prohibits from the start.[4]

No wonder theology put the lid on *tehom*! But it got out again, just in time for the twentieth century, with its awesome mix of both creative and destructive chaos. Gunkel absorbed for "Old Testament" studies the shock of new excavations of mythological parallels to the story of creation from primal waters. The Babylonian *Enuma Elish* presented eerie echoes of both structure and symbolism. And there emerged therein the etymological link of *tehom* to *Tiamat*, the Sumerian-Semitic term for the watery chaos. The feminine *tehom* is used in Gen. 1:2 without an article, like a proper name. It was recognized now to allude to Tiamat, who "before anything was named" mingled her waters with her mate "Apsu." From them the gods precipitate. But Apsu wants to kill the noisy grandchildren ("I want to sleep!"). Tiamat protests in agony, "Shall we destroy what we have created?" "Yes," she laments, "their way is difficult, but let us take it goodnaturedly."[5] The grandchildren kill him first. Immersed in the mythic version of clinical depression, Tiamat then gets in touch with her anger. Breeding monsters, she morphs into the Babylonian mascot of evil. The great warrior Marduk, chief god of Babylon, today's Baghdad, becomes Lord through his gory slaughter of the Grand Mother. From her bleeding corpse he constructs the universe, in the sequence that Genesis echoes—Genesis being composed during or just after the Babylonian exile. To him the emperors of Babylon would "appeal in terms of strength." Out of what Babylonian body parts is today's global order being composed?[6]

Is Tehom a priestly allusion to Tiamat, and Marduk to Yahweh? Appalled at such possible derivation from this pagan chaos, Barth decided that the second verse does not refer to God's Spirit at all. This "impotent bird" fluttering over "sterile waters" must be a parody of mythology, of the "monstrous world" of chaos to which God said "No" from the beginning. Other interpreters have taken the unveiled mythic chaos more seriously. They draw on divine warrior motifs (especially in Isaiah and the Psalms) to make a strong case that (a) God is a divine warrior, (b) the chaos is evil itself, and (c) God creates and redeems *not from nothing* but from the struggle with the chaos (for example, Frank Moore Cross, Bernard Batto, Jon Levenson). In other words, both Jewish and Christian interpreters discover in Gen. 1:2 a quiet replay of creation by murder. Is *this* then the mystery of the lost chaos? Must it be hidden because it echoes a bloody pagan warrior myth?

Certainly there are biblical texts that demonize the deep and its monsters: "You divided the sea by your might; you broke the heads of the dragons in the waters. You crushed the heads of Leviathan" (Ps. 74:13-14). This is a poignant theopolitical response to invasion by Babylon. It symptomatizes an approach I have called *tehomophobia*. For women at least, it would hardly represent an improvement over the *ex nihilo* theology.

She-Monsters

As the primal feminine waters reflect the saltwaters of the womb, so the warrior-ethos is based on a cosmic matricide. We already of course presume that the Hebrews absorbed the patriarchy of the environment, that biblical monotheism therefore inevitably made God male, that the divine warrior does recur in the Bible, preeminently in the Apocalypse. There Tiamat, the horror of Babylon, appears as the Whore of Babylon, and salvation means "no more sea." For transparently gendered motives, I have been tracking this good monster for a couple of decades. Feminist writer Robin Morgan's refrain—"I am a monster/and I am proud"—chants in my mind whenever I hear of great warriors, gods or men, slaying their various dragons.

The resurrecting of Tiamat/Tehom is therefore one symbolic strategy for the becoming of women. If *genesis* means becoming, it reverberates in Alice Jardine's lovely neologism, *gynesis*: woman as a process, not a fixed nature or subject. The biblical genesis carries the trace of an unfulfilled gynesis. Luce Irigaray has exposed points at which the oceanic has been repressed along with, indeed elementally inseparable from, the depth and power of women in our civilization. In her gyno-poetic medium she asks, "Fluid and flaming as she is, are they not eager to dry her up?"[7] I think we all know this dried-up condition. And particularly we know how women have often acquiesced in a desiccated, tense, shrunken version of who we might have been, of who we might yet become—if we flow and flame.

So a theopoetics of becoming remembers among its *dramatis personae* this Tiamat, primal female creator, who morphed into the original "fe-monster." But this is not to claim of the chaos itself that it is inherently *good*. In Gen. 1:2, "the great sea monsters" materialize prominently at the culmination of an emphatically *good* creation. By contrast, the *Enuma Elish* never calls the creation "good," nor does it even fill it with nonhuman life; and certainly no "man and woman" pair appear in its epic narrative, to tantalize history for millennia with the prospect of a gendered equality.

· Will the Real Leviathan Please . . . Breach?

Sea monsters lurk in the margins of our realities. You've probably seen premodern maps with dragons drawn at the edges of the known world: *hic seunt dracones* (here there be dragons!). In the boundary zones of the other, the dark, the native, and the strange, the dream demons could be kept at a distance. But when the world itself is set on edge, the chaos monsters reappear. And politically they come in handy. For instance, in the speech that first made public the new doctrine of preemptive force, President Bush three times invoked the chaos:

> The attacks of September the 11th required a few hundred thousand dollars in the hands of a few dozen evil and deluded men. All of the *chaos* and suffering they caused came at much less than the cost of a single tank. . . . [Deterrence and] containment [are] not possible when unbalanced dictators with weapons of mass destruction can deliver those weapons on missiles or secretly provide them to terrorist allies. . . . We will lift this dark threat from our country and from the world. . . . More and more, civilized nations find ourselves on the same side—*united by common dangers of terrorist violence and chaos.* . . . When the great powers share common values, we are better able . . . to cooperate in preventing the spread of violence or *economic chaos.*[8]

Thus we behold a strangely postmodern, flexible, many-headed monster, with now a Saudi, now an Afghan, now a Palestinian, now an Iraqi face. If the pretension of world unity against the WMD-armed monster proved ludicrous, nonetheless, it supports Zygmunt Bauman's prediction of global space assuming "the character of a frontier-land."[9] Postmodern politics will abolish the maps of the modern nation state. For the dark terrorist threat will be as transnational as its imperial enemy—it will appear everywhere and nowhere. The dragons are no longer confined to the margins of the mapped cosmos, and now their threat of chaos legitimates the sovereignty of the first truly global empire. A lead article in *The Atlantic Monthly* even offered rules for conducting this "American imperium": "For the time being," wrote journalist Robert Kaplan, "the highest morality must be the preservation—and wherever prudent, the accretion—of American power." The highest morality is amoral power? How does one back such doublespeak? According to Kaplan, only our power can establish order at this "*dangerous and chaotic moment* in world history."[10] With such chaos-monsters of formless terror, we can freely choose our enemies.

The theorists of the present regime have solid historical precedent. We have heard their successful advocacy of the philosophy of Thomas Hobbes (see chapter 2), who held that however much destruction the state sovereignty inflicts, it is always superior to the alternative, defined, of course, as chaos or the war of all against all. So the state's might is not only its right; given the threat of chaos, might *is* right. Leviathan must be thwarted, or . . . wait. That is not the way Hobbes's Leviathan works; it does not at all correspond to its biblical antecedent. Hobbes calls Leviathan the "godlike champion of order against chaos."[11] His Leviathan is the *state*, not the anarchy it subdues! Hobbes was hardly ignorant of his sources but carefully cited the culminating vision from Job's whirlwind, Leviathan as God's favorite, the one who is "king over the proud." This early modern theopolitics shaped western imperial politics. In Hobbes's twisted exegesis of Job we glimpse the (il)logic of theopolitics: an all-powerful order is always preferable to "chaos," even if the order proves to *be* the very monster of chaos! This is divine omnipotence morphed into secular politics. With it come all the contradictions of theodicy, of the attempt to call good that which causes evil. So if the ideal state *is* the Leviathan, redefined as the violent imposition of order, then no wonder the destructive chaos produced, for example, by the United States in Iraq can be scripted as the creation of order, since order after all is the most violent monster. Some of Hobbes's contemporaries were appalled at his justification of the lawless arrogance of the state as a "monster of hegemony."[12] Yet Job's Leviathan suggests neither the terrorizing hegemony of a state nor the terrorist extremities of resistance.

Many exegetes only hear in the whirlwind speech the thundering boasts of a bully God, whose culminating description of two monsters serves just to shame and silence poor suffering Job. That reading works—if you ignore most of the content of God's speech. It is a leading ecological writer and activist who perhaps best brings Job to current life. He hears the voice calling us, "overwhelmingly, to joy. To immersion in the fantastic beauty and drama all around us." So writes Bill McKibben. "The reason Job matters so much to me is because of the language—the biologically accurate, earthy, juicy, crusty, wild, untamed poetry of God's great speech."[13] Indeed it is this voice that also asked, "Where were you when I stopped the waters, as they issued gushing from the womb? When I wrapped the ocean in clouds and swaddled the sea in shadows? When I closed it in with barriers and set its boundaries, saying 'here you may come, but no farther'?"[14] An amazing image—not of a terrifying sea monster but of a squalling infant bursting forth in amniotic liquidity, to be held and diapered by the Ineffable.

Most interpreters still insist, however, that the epiphany is all about "the power of the Creator." I think it is less about force and more about farce. I think it caricatures what was already in Job's time conventional tehomophobic piety. As one Hebrew Bible scholar notes, "the image is deliberately absurd: this violent chaos monster is but an infant, born from a womb, wrapped in baby clothes and placed in a playpen."[15] The boundaries are set not in patriarchal command rhetoric, but rather in loving protection, in an embrace that allows the world to develop. Scholars wonder nervously about that womb that apparently precedes any creation. Whose is it? The Qumran Targum on Job 38:8 reads that "it gushed from the womb of the deep [*rehem tehom*]."[16] Does that genitive mean that the *tehom has* the womb or *is* the womb? If the tehom is uncreated, the question remains: Whose womb is it?

Job says that he had only heard by ear, whereas now he *sees*. But the vision does not display any features at all of God. The voice does not display God in abstraction but rather through the vision of the wild creatures of the creation. Does Job realize in retrospect that to "see" God *is* to see the creation? To see the *body of God*—womb and all, the all that spills forth so chaotically, so creatively, so procreatively? Yet this epiphany does not deprive God of agency, or reduce *Elohim* to the impersonal force of nature. As feminist biblical scholar Carol Newsome writes, "This new image is one of God as a power for life, balancing the needs of all creatures, not just humans, cherishing freedom, full of fierce love and delight for each thing without regard for its utility, acknowledging the deep interconnectedness of death and life, restraining and nurturing each element in the ecology of all creation." She hardly needs add that "it is a description of God and the world that has strong points of contact with contemporary feminist thought"[17]—at least with the feminist theology that is worth its salt. Rosemary Radford Ruether's Divine Matrix that is sea-salty with interconnection suggests womb as matter/*mater* (Latin for "mother"). Sallie McFague's universe as the "body of God" suggests the radically incarnational *nature* of that God. For nature is after all the natal, the birth-giving site of all creation. Thus Ivone Gebara proposes the expression "esse-diversity of God"—to invoke "the relatedness of everything with everything else," to signify that the being (Latin: *esse*) of God is not that of a transcendent and self-same ontology but rather "that reality that penetrates, crosses and vivifies every other reality, beyond any good or evil named and carried out by human beings."[18]

The poet of Job reinscribes the monster upon the whirlwind context of its greatest epiphany. Whirlwinds in meteorology are complex chaotic systems that suggest not pure chaos but rather the turbulent emergence of complexity at the edge of chaos. I am standing with Job on a certain hermeneutical edge of the tradition, insisting that the Bible offers something more than the tehomophobic tradition. There is also its *tehomophilic* strand. And this presents itself not just in the Book of Job.

> O Lord, how manifold are your works!
> In wisdom you have made them all; . . .
> Yonder is the sea, great and wide,
> creeping things innumerable are there,
> living things both small and great.
> There go the ships,
> and Leviathan that you formed to sport in it.
> (Ps. 104:24-26)

Theopoetic Connections

We have swum here with three related schools of tehomic monster. We might (in the sporting spirit) dub them femonsters, islamonsters, ecomonsters. But they are shifting exemplifications or projections of a primal relation, an originative connection to the chaos. That connection may be repressed, as in the *ex nihilo* doctrine; it may be feared, as in the tehomophobic trajectory. Or it may be in a risky and ultimately creative sense embraced. I have argued that Genesis 1 belongs to the latter, the tehomophilic trajectory. Let us return to the first chapter of the Bible, with the help of Rashi, who wrote of the chaos verse: "This verse cries out, 'interpret me!'" This eleventh-century Jewish interpreter insisted that Gen. 1:1 is not a sentence, but a dependent clause: (1) *As* in the beginning God was creating the heaven and the earth, (2) *then* the earth was *tohuvabohu* and the darkness upon the face of the deep and the spirit of God was moving on the waters—(3) *then* God said, "Let there be light." Rashi's inference? The *"text does not intend to point out the order of the acts of Creation*—to state that these (heaven and earth) were created first."[19] So the translation itself breaks up the idea of a linear sequence. Already a bit of syntactical turbulence disturbs what Claus Westermann lauded as "the effective monotone" of Genesis 1. Several recent translations follow Rashi (NRSV, New Jewish). But of course once the linear order is broken up, the entire process of creation reads as *co-creation*: God has the waters and the earth after all do their own producing (vv. 20, 24) and calls the "great sea monsters"—Job's Leviathan—good! Might we sense here too the survival of a *tehomophilic* tradition?

Then feel again the intimate vibration of God the Spirit upon the face of the deep: not as a polytheistic regression, but as a *theopolitical* repudiation of the Marduk style of imperial Order. Might *tehom* signify an unrealized depth of reality, an infinite *theopoetic* potentiality that may become good or evil in its actualizations but is the "stuff" from which all things come? Would it then return us to Christian thinkers like Hermogenes, who thought constructively with the *khora*, the formless place or third space from which all things arise, in Plato's *Timaeus*? This *khora* is being creatively reread by theorists such as Julia Kristeva as a rhythmic embodiment of relation to the mother, by Derrida as the place of difference itself, and by postcolonial theory as the "third space," the boundary zone.

How does complex order arise from such chaos? Chaos theorists refer to "the irony of turbulence." Chaos—which is *not disorder* but a complex pattern of turbulent fragmentation, containing an alternative, an *other*, nonlinear order—arises in nature from "the system's *infinitely deep interconnectedness*."[20] That infinitely deep interconnectedness comes close to what in process theology is conceived as the "extensive continuum," the matrix in which everything is interrelated in the relativity of the universe. But the continuum of relations does not exist statically, like a fishnet.

Rather, all your relations are a potential for your next moment of becoming (genesis), and *your* becoming *now* is potential for the future becomings of your world. This is the potentiality that has been imagined as a frightening chaos. Indeed it can flood; it can overwhelm. All our relations can drown our individuality. And there are also the relations of violence and fear. Together they stimulate desire for the redeeming warrior. But because of the inescapably reciprocal character of the continuum of relations, the warrior messiah who comes to clean up the world's evil ends up making his own bloody mess: hence the "Son" whose Word incinerates the unbelievers, producing the apocalyptic body count in which the popular *Left Behind* novels revel.

Creatio ex Profundis

There is undeniable tehomophobia in some especially embattled biblical contexts (like Psalm 74, Isaiah, and of course Revelation). That, I believe, is the motif that was taken postbiblically to its logical conclusion in the *creatio ex nihilo,* which brands the chaos as an absolute nothingness. Of course the potentiality of materiality *tohuvabohu*, of the infinitely deep interconnectedness of *tehom*, may indeed from a certain perspective be called "nothing"—no thing at all, like the Buddhist no-thingness. The *creatio ex nihilo* is one possible theological interpretation of scripture, and it can itself be interpreted in many ways. I am suggesting not that we dispose of it but that we complement

it by another hermeneutic, one we may call the *creatio ex profundis*. This
phrase emphasizes the *depth* more than its chaos as such; the womb-watery potentiality of becoming is never merely chaos, in the sense of sheer disorder. Its profundity is not a vertical dimension but the multidimensional continuum of all relations, the continuum from which order, cosmos, continually emerges: *creatio continuo*. Thus the creation as genesis is not reducible either to chaos or to cosmos. Let us call it by James Joyce's fabulous neologism: the *chaosmos*.

How does God as *Elohim*, as Word or Wisdom, relate to the *tehom*, if it is already always there? Is it an eternal Other? Wouldn't this be a two-God dualism or ditheism? This would be as misleading as the nonrelational monism of an omnipotent God, who, we are supposed to imagine, suddenly, after an eternity of self-absorption, decided to make a world.

Instead of a dividing line between God and the chaos, we might imagine—as this scripture does—a mysterious darkness. A darkness not of opacity, for the light has not yet been separated out of it. The light, like every luminary we see in the formed universe, is *in* the darkness. So the fifteenth-century cardinal Nicholas of Cusa offered a radical notion of the divine. This whom we worship "as inaccessible light is not light whose opposite is darkness, but is light, in which *darkness is infinite light*."[21] Light and dark in this mystical tradition are not opposites. And the pre-creation light symbolizes a state that is not just cosmological but epistemological: the darkness over the face of the deep is the darkness of our own unknowing. As the seventeenth-century poet Henry Vaughan wrote,

> There is in God (some say)
> A deep, but dazzling darkness. . . .[22]

Might we imagine *tehom* as that very dark and dazzling depth—the profundity and womb of God? Not "the same" as God—who, as the trinity hints, is internally complex precisely *as* eternally relational, not simply self-same, self-identical—but as the Other in God's self, like the Godhead of the mystics? In this infinity we find ourselves in over our heads, always, but never out of our depths! There is no way out. For space and time themselves unfold from within this *tehom*.

Can a tehomic theology help our culture outgrow the violent certainties and messianic innocence of its "simple faith"? Is Christianity not recognizing that it has participated in wars and horrors and terrors beyond telling, indeed in violence against the creation itself? That we participate in the very de-creation of heaven and earth? Might our communities cease to deface the dark face of the deep? Christians have demonized every mysterious Other that they could mark as *dark*—sexual, ethnic, racial, religious. We have perpetrated a *light* supremacism. "In the shadows of late night," writes bell hooks of a conversation with her sister, "we talk about the need to see darkness differently."[23] This is a socially embodied need—and a mystical lure. Might we live more co-creatively, more *becomingly*, amid the shadows and the chaos—the uncertainty, unpredictability, turbulence, and complexity—of our own lives? our souls? our sexualities? our communities? our cultures? the other cultures among us and beyond us? the ecologies in which human culture is so ungratefully and now precariously embedded?

If we read our complex connections not in terms of cuts but of folds (and *complex* comes, after all, from the Latin for "folded together"), then we are working not in terms of absolute differences but of differential relations. Thus we find ourselves practicing the third genre, the theopolitical *khora,* that opens the "interstitial perspective" of postcolonial theory. No wonder that perspective begins to open out from within, as in Spivak's "animist liberation theology," to include the wisdom of those peoples closest to nonhuman nature, indeed to work—in an almost impossible breadth of love—for the decolonization of the planet itself. And here the "indeconstructibility of justice" (Derrida) unfolds not at bottom from the negations of an angry either/or but from a positively pluralizing love. Thus Trinh T. Minh-ha writes, discussing June Jordan, "The struggle of positionalities may in the end be said to depend upon the accurate tuning of one's many selves. *Where is the love?*"[24] For the plurality of our relations to a complex world requires attunement each to our own complexity: the multiplicity of the world is both within and without. So this sort of fluid positionality is a kind of spiritual practice, always as internal as it is external, as personal as it is political. Thus it comes charged with a certain theological eros, the intimacy of the spirit vibrating upon the face of the waters.

Can we grant ourselves and each other such breathing room? Does the breezy *rûach* (Hebrew for "spirit") not even now vibrate on the waters of our lived lives? When divinity "speaks," does it perhaps do so through the Word that is Wisdom, the Sophia at the edges of our understanding? Is it she who in us becomes the human wisdom Cusa calls the *knowing ignorance*, the great uncertainty principle of theology? Or as Gebara more recently wrote "out of the depths," "We believe in the dimension of 'not-knowing,' a fundamental dimension of our being, a not-knowing that makes us more humble and at the same time more combative, in order to gain respect for differences and the possibility of building an interdependent society." In this profound ecofeminist theology unknowing means not relativism but wisdom: "We look for a Wisdom in life, a Wisdom that teaches us to share our goods and the goods of the earth, so as not to have any 'needy person' among us (Acts 4:34)."[25] The theopolitics of uncertainty is precisely not lacking in ethical clarity.

Granted, many people come to faith precisely in order to escape uncertainty. And the modalities of fundamentalism across the religions will continue to promise certainty. They offer a cure for the ambiguity of life. Oldstream Christianity, let alone the mystical paths of any religion, cannot ever compete on the terrain of certainty. There we simply lose. Indeed we might despair at a so-called Christian public who supports a politics of religious certainty—even, to return to the starting point of this chapter, presidents who claim to know and do the will of their God-Father. This certainty has permitted the new messianic imperialism. But given the manifest failure of its projects, we need not despair. Its certainty proves certainly wrong. Its promises of stability and order are exposed as reckless boasts. And many who had been blinded by the light of a false certainty learn to see in the dark. The space opens wider, then, for Wisdom, in whom we learn the humbling old knowledge of our own ignorance.

Theopoetics and Theopolitics

This unknowing throws us back upon faith, not as an absolute kind of knowledge, but as the trustful courage that we require precisely *because* we cannot have certainty. Because we are always beginning again. This would not be a confessionalism that stifles our questions. Faith is the opposite of fundamentalism. It thrives in the spirit of a *theopoetics* that flows beneath and beyond our *theopolitics*. For we can in a sense solve the murderous mystery of the abuse of power in the name of divine omnipotence. It is theology as mystification. But our theopoetics poses a mystery that we do not solve but can only embrace—not that the embrace is comfortable. It may be the experience not of beauty but of evil that provokes a poetic transmutation of theology: "Talk that is not absolute or so certain seems more suitable to these difficult times," writes Gebara, working among the poorest of Brazil, of difficulty sealed in by the empire to the north. "Poetic language, which reveals and hides things at the same time, seems better fitted to heal our wounds and to help us search out, in this age of common tragedy, new ways to learn to live together." I suspect poetic language has been better fitted to heal the theopolitical violence of any age. For in every age the wounds inflicted by certainty—and perhaps in ours more totally, more globally—will be better healed by a discourse of uncertainty than by just another sure truth. A counter-apocalyptic truth is all the more truthful because it does not cease to question itself. But it will be a truth in the making, a risk-taking creativity rather than a reckless absolute. "We may not avoid mistakes in the search, but we must always dare to have creativity."[26] Creativity and the questions that clear the path for it: these have not been recognized until recently as primary modalities of faith, and so of theology.

The more we ask, search, and test our answers, the deeper the questions take us. Yet as the questions deepen, the answers that we gather do not simply crumble; only the false certainties do that. This deepening process is not just about voiding, emptying, and deconstructing. Rather, the emptying out, the kenosis of prior meanings, lets precisely the immense, sparkling dimensionality of life into our awareness. We might say that it lets us share a hint, a facet, of the divine perspective upon the universe. We cannot then occupy a God's-eye view, but we can glimpse, imagine, and remember its unfathomable expanse. Thus we let the poetics of divine life glance like a psalm upon our daily lives, upon the trivial pursuits in which we build up a life. This building up is only an illusion if we fantasize for it unshakeable foundations. In a faith free of the fantasy of certainty, we build lives and politics and perhaps a new planet on the firmest ground we can find—but in sight of the shoreline, the edge of chaos, where the next big certainty is being washed out at this very moment. Precisely because of its uncertainty principle, then, a theology of becoming is not a process of voiding, of answer-avoidance, but of gathering our relations and our resources into fresh and flowing compositions. We let go, and we also "pile up" (the root meaning of "construct"). A constructive theology of becoming deconstructs the delusions of a simple answer, a simple self, a simple God. But it does not leave a mere rubble of relativism. Instead it piles up and folds together, in the incarnate complexity of an animate creation, the potentialities of this very moment.

Amid the chaosmos of our relations, the particularity of this time, this place, reveals itself with a new vividness. It invites novelty of response; indeed, it invites the fullest sense of H. Richard Niebuhr's "responsible self," a self that is able to respond activates because of its receptivity to the other. And as heirs of the biblical tradition, we understand this self always to be responsible to God, responsive to the divine call. This is precisely not to confuse our delusions of omnipotence with divine fatherhood and to blame our violence upon God. It is to recognize the bottomless difference between the human and the divine. Does this faith render us passive—and thus after all irresponsible? apolitical? Precisely not: the wisdom of uncertainty releases the courage of faith. And that faith is the confidence to act in the face of an open-ended future, thus to act in great humility and in great love. It enables us to throw ourselves into a planetary struggle for "justice, peace and the integrity of creation." It enables us to sustain this struggle creatively, knowing that creation itself is a chaosmos of new beginnings. The practice of creation from and in the chaos is an exercise of strength with "extreme sensitivity to initial conditions."

The creation is not then a timeline running from absolute beginning to absolute closure. That power-line has been encouraging irresponsible empire-building and predatory globalization, which inflicts an order from above, an order based not on sustainability but on exploitation. For its timeline is always running out. Its deformed apocalypse lets it use up the world because Father will create us a new one. What an infantile fantasy of greed and omnipotence grips our collective unconscious. But somehow simultaneously we do not cease as a species to mature. The resistance is immense and growing. It is learning the wisdom of "extreme sensitivity," of a creative, coalitional eros that weaves strength from multiple sites of weakness. So a constructive theology of becoming sustains a political theology of love. Love can weave its way between justice and uncertainty, at the edge of any chaos. Within a religious context, we may call the way, the love, and the mystery: "God." If God ceases to be a poetic invocation, however, and begins to control the political context, we have no longer to do with the God of love, but with the idol of omnipotence.

Instead of solving and dissolving the mystery, we may begin to practice a theopoetics of the flowing shoreline, where the waves refract the interplay of darkness and dazzle. We may more gracefully become co-creators in the flowing image of one who creates *ex profundis*.

A mystic of the Baroque era put the mystery in a drop of poetry:

> In a droplet—say how can this be?—
> The whole ocean of God flows into me.[27]

Acknowledgments

Over the last several years I have developed the ideas in this book in many lectures, presentations, and publications. Although the ideas and presentation of them are further developed here, I wish to acknowledge with gratitude those institutions and publishers who have sponsored my work in their prior versions and iterations.

Chapter 1, "The Armageddon of 9/11," revisits work published in *Strike Terror No More: Theology, Ethics, and the New War*, ed. Jon L. Berquist (St. Louis: Chalice, 2002).

Chapter 2, "Preemption and Omnipotence," was delivered at Drew Transdisciplinary Theological Colloquium II: An American Empire, September, 2003.

Chapter 5, "Eyes All Over" reworks ideas I also broached in "Eyeing the Apocalypse," in *Postmodern Interpretations of the Bible: A Reader*, ed. A. K. M. Adam (St. Louis: Chalice, 2000).

Chapter 6, "Everywhere and Nowhere" was presented at the Second Drew Transdisciplinary Theological Colloquium I: Com/Promised Lands, September 2002. A version of these ideas also appeared in "The Love of Postcolonialism: Theology in the Interstices of Empire," *Postcolonial Theologies: Divinity and Empire*, ed. Catherine Keller, Michael Nausner, and Mayra Rivera (St. Louis: Chalice, 2004).

Notes

1. The Armageddon of 9/11: Lament for the New Millennium

1. Edward W. Said, "The Clash of Ignorance," *The Nation*, October 22, 2001, 11–13.

2. I propose "counter-apocalypse" as an alternative to both un–self-critical "apocalypticism," which tends to literalize the prophetic voice, and to "anti-apocalypse," which represses it; see my book *Apocalypse Now and Then: A Feminist Guide to the End of the World* (Boston: Beacon, 1996).

3. I am not in a position to invent new terminology for the twentieth-century literalist or absolutist branch of Islam, and indeed I seek to solicit its non-otherness by use of the term *fundamentalist*. But I use it with the following, pre-9/11 proviso in mind: "So long as the Western world . . . anxiously follows the spread of the Islamic movements incorrectly termed 'fundamentalist' (Islam, with all its different faces, cannot be blanketed under the single term 'fundamentalist'), there exists in Europe a widespread tendency to view Islam as a potential adversary." Franco Cardini, *Europe and Islam*, trans. Caroline Beamish, *The Making of Europe* (Oxford: Blackwell, 2001), 1.

4. Norman O. Brown, "The Apocalypse of Islam," *Apocalypse and/or Metamorphosis* (Berkeley: University of California Press, 1991), 86.

5. Sura 70, "The Stairways," *The Koran Interpreted*, trans. Arthur J. Arberry, (New York: Macmillan, 1955), 300.

6. Sura 16, v. 77.

7. "The City," to which the founding *hejirah*, or "migration," was made by him and his community of believers in 622.

8. The five pillars comprise the fundamental practices of Islam. The first is the *Shhada*, or witness ("There is no god but God," *la ilaha illa'llah*) and "Muham-

mad is God's messenger." The second is the *Salat*, or ritual prayer; the third is giving to the needy; the fourth is fasting during the month of Ramadan; the fifth is the Hajj to Mecca. "Behind all the stress on practice is the recognition that the Koran must become flesh and blood. It is not enough for people to read the Koran or learn what it says. They have to embody the Book." Sachiko Murata and William C. Chittick, *The Vision of Islam* (St. Paul: Paragon, 1994), 9.

9. "Where Christians discerned God's hand in apparent failure and defeat, when Jesus died on the cross, Muslims experienced political success as sacramental and as a revelation of the divine presence in their lives. It is important, however, to be clear that when the Arabs burst out of Arabia they were not impelled by the ferocious power of 'Islam.'" Karen Armstrong, *Islam: A Short History* (New York: Random House, 2000), 29. I recommend this readable text for an introduction.

10. "After the campaigns waged by the caliphs who immediately succeeded the Prophet, that is from the 630's onwards, the expansion of Islam never resembled an inexorable military conquest. . . . It was in fact a continuous, not always consistent process of conversion . . . of groups belonging to exhausted or crisis-ridden societies—for example the Monophysite Christians of Syria and Egypt, harshly treated by the basileus of Byzantium. . . . Many nevertheless preferred to remain loyal to their own faith . . . and to be considered as *dhimmi*—'protected' as well as 'subject.' They there by demonstrated, incidentally, their opinion of government by the infidel as being preferable to government by their co-religionists." Cardini, *Europe and Islam*, 4.

11. For a study of the highly gendered and spatialized apocalypticism of Christopher Columbus as constitutive of "modernity," see Catherine Keller, "The Breast, the Apocalypse and the Colonial Journey," in *The Year 2000: Essays on the End*, ed. Charles B. Strozier and Michael Flynn (New York: New York University Press, 1997), 42–58, or my *Apocalypse Now and Then*, 140–80.

12. "He is known to have discussed Voltaire's Mahomet with Goethe, and to have defended Islam and the Prophet. His interest in the East was accompanied by a strong sympathy with the crusades." Cardini, *Europe and Islam*, 197.

13. In the process he maintained the support of the Ottoman Empire by defeating the Wahabite sect of Arabia, whose brand of Islam is still a key stream of contemporary Muslim missions in the West and extremism in the Middle East.

14. Al-Jabarti, early nineteenth-century sheikh, cited in Karen Armstrong, *The Battle for God* (New York: Ballantine, 2000), 113.

15. Led by Hasan al-Banna (1906–1949) until his assassination, the Brothers (as well as Sisters) sought freedom and dignity from European cultural dominance and economic destitution. Suppressed through mass imprisonment, torture, and extermination of Brothers by Jaml Abd al-Nasser, the Brotherhood became a militant underground movement.

16. Thus Ayatollah Kashani prophesied at the time, marking the emergence of the United States as a colonial aggressor. "When Iranians looked back on Operation Ajax, they would forget the defection of their own people from Musad-

diq, and believe implicitly that the United States had single-handedly imposed the shah's dictatorship upon them. . . . There seemed to be a double standard. America proudly proclaimed its belief in freedom and democracy, but warmly supported a shah who permitted no opposition to his rule, and denied Iranians fundamental human rights." Armstrong, *Battle for God*, 229. This double standard was already becoming standard international policy.

17. "Nobody had ever claimed before that jihad was equivalent to the five Pillars of Islam, but Mawdudi felt that the innovation was justified by the present emergency. The stress and fear of cultural and religious annihilation had led to the development of a more extreme and potentially violent distortion of the faith." Ibid., 168.

18. "Qutb told Muslims to model themselves on Muhammad: to separate themselves from mainstream society (as Muhammad had made the hijrah from Mecca to Medina), and then engage in a violent jihad. But Muhammad had in fact finally achieved victory by an ingenious policy of non-violence; the Quran adamantly opposed force and coercion in religious matters, and its vision—far from preaching exclusion and separation—was tolerant and inclusive. Qutb insisted that the Quranic injunction to tolerance could occur only after the political victory of Islam and the establishment of a true Muslim state." Ibid., 169–70.

19. See especially Leila Ahmed, *Women and Gender in Islam: Historical Roots of a Modern Debate* (New Haven: Yale University Press, 1992).

20. Armstrong, *Islam*, 165.

21. Gustav Niebuhr, "Finding Fault: U.S. Secular Groups Set Tone for Terror Attacks, Falwell Says," *New York Times*, September 14, 2001, A18.

22. Ibid.

23. For a succinct guide to the theological and postmodern problematic of "modernity," I recommend Paul Lakeland, *Postmodernity: Christian Identity in a Fragmented Age*, Guides to Theological Inquiry (Minneapolis: Fortress Press, 1997).

24. See Walter Wink, *Engaging the Powers: Discernment and Resistance in a World of Domination* (Minneapolis: Fortress Press, 1992).

25. Eva Hoffman has given sarcastic voice to my discomfort: "Still, the instant deflection of rage from the perpetrator to the target, the undercurrent of schadenfreude evident in many statements ('What do you expect, given American foreign policy? They had it coming to them. We have to have a more complex view of where terrorist rage comes from. Americans will just have to learn why the world hates them so much') has been astonishing and dismaying. . . . The first impulse of many progressive commentators in the wake of the terrible events was to reach for their holsters and come up brandishing standard-issue anti-Americanism as if it were a brave new piece of subversive analysis." *The Independent* (online edition), September 27, 2001, www.independent.co.uk.

26. Edward Said notes that there is "as yet no decent history or demystification" of this contest of the three, whose "bloody modern convergence on Pales-

tine furnishes a rich secular instance of what has been so tragically irreconcilable about them. Not surprisingly, then, Muslims and Christians speak readily of crusades and jihads, both of them eliding the Judaic presence with often sublime insouciance." Said, "The Clash of Ignorance," 13.

2. Preemption and Omnipotence: A Niebuhrian Prophecy

1. As Richard W. Van Alstyne has written: "In reality, . . . the United States possesses the attributes of monarchy; and it is through the President, the elective king, that it exerts its sovereign will among the family of nations. William H. Seward, Lincoln's Secretary of State, saw all this at a glance . . . and said: 'We elect a king for four years, and give him absolute power within certain limits, which after all he can interpret for himself'" (*The Rising American Empire* [New York: Norton, 1960], 6).

2. "Remarks by the President at 2002 Graduation Exercise of the United States Military Academy, West Point, New York," Office of the Press Secretary, June 1, 2002. My argument will not preclude the possible defensive necessity of forms of preemptive strike, *if* "imminent danger" were to be actually established.

3. Edward Said, "The Nation Is Not United: The Other America," *Counter-Punch* (March 21, 2003): 3.

4. Reinhold Niebuhr, *The Irony of American History* (New York: Scribner's, 1952), 38.

5. Ibid., 24.

6. George W. Bush, 2002 State of the Union Address, cited in "Bush & God," *Newsweek*, March 10, 2003.

7. See Catherine Keller, "The Armageddon of 9/11: A Counter-Apocalyptic Meditation," in *Strike Terror No More: Theology, Ethics, and the New War*, ed. Jon L. Berquist (St. Louis: Chalice, 2002). For an analysis of the theopolitics of the Book of Revelation, see my *Apocalypse Now and Then: A Feminist Guide to the End of the World* (Boston: Beacon, 1996).

8. Alfred North Whitehead, *Process and Reality*, Corrected Edition, ed. David Ray Griffin and Donald W. Sherburne (New York: Free Press, 1978), 342.

9. Raymund of Aguiles, July 15, 1099, quoted in August C. Krey, *The First Crusade: The Accounts of Eye-Witnesses and Participants* (Princeton: Princeton University Press, 1921), 261–62. For a more readable account of the Crusades and the other Abrahamic forms of messianic militarism, see Karen Armstrong, *Holy Wars: The Crusades and Their Impact on Today's World* (New York: Knopf, 2001).

10. Rahul Mahajan, *New Crusade: America's War on Terrorism* (New York: Monthly Review Press, 2002), 104.

11. Cited in Niall Ferguson's informatively pro-imperial text, *Empire: The Rise and Demise of the British World Order and the Lessons for Global Power* (New York: Basic Books, 2002), 7.

12. Lawrence F. Kaplan and William Kristol, *The War over Iraq: Saddam's Tyranny and America's Mission* (San Francisco: Encounter, 2003), 109–11.

13. On the U.S. government's nefarious role in these (and many other countries), see William Blum, *Killing Hope: U.S. Military and CIA Interventions since World War II* (Monroe, Maine: Common Courage, 1995).

14. Kaplan and Kristol, *The War over Iraq*, 115.

15. Ibid., 3.

16. Niebuhr, *The Irony of American History*, 143.

17. Tariq Ali, *The Clash of Fundamentalisms: Crusades, Jihads and Modernity* (London: Verso, 2002), 1. "Politically," says Ali, "the United States decided early on to use the tragedy [9/11] as a moral lever to re-map the world" (xiii).

18. David Ray Griffin, *God, Power, and Evil: A Process Theodicy* (Louisville: Westminster John Knox, 2004 [1976]).

19. John Calvin, *Institutes of the Christian Religion*, III.xxiii.1, I.xviii.1.

20. *The National Security Strategy of the United States of America*, September 17, 2002; available at: http://www.whitehouse.gov/nsc/nss.html.

21. Calvin, *Institutes*, III.xii.1.

22. Kaplan and Kristol, *The War over Iraq*, 3. Foreign policy expert Joshua Muravchick's logic is revealing: "A policeman gets his assignments from higher authority, but in the community of nations there is no authority higher than America" (cited with approval in Kaplan and Kristol, *The War over Iraq*, 121). This is a vision that Calvin would have denounced as idolatry—precisely for its aping of the omnipotent authority.

23. Calvin, *Institutes*, III.xiii.7.

24. Ibid., I.vii.8.

25. Kaplan and Kristol, *The War over Iraq*, 123.

26. Niebuhr, *The Irony of American History*, 50.

27. Calvin, as quoted by Niebuhr, who is considering Max Weber's interpretation of Calvinism in *The Protestant Ethic and the Spirit of Capitalism*. Ibid., 51.

28. William Stoughton (then president of Yale University), "New England's True Interest," cited in Niebuhr, *The Irony of American History*, 51.

29. Ibid., 146.

30. Whitehead, *Process and Reality*, 342.

31. Griffin, *God, Power, and Evil*.

32. Introductory versions of these movements in theology include: John B. Cobb Jr and David Ray Griffin, *Process Theology: An Introductory Exposition* (Philadelphia: Westminster, 1976); Charles Hartshorne, *Omnipotence and Other Theological Mistakes* (Albany: State University of New York, 1984); Marjorie Suchocki, *God, Christ, Church: A Practical Guide to Process Theology*, rev. ed. (New York: Crossroad, 1989); Sallie McFague, *The Body of God: An Ecological Theology* (Minneapolis: Fortress Press, 1993) and *Super, Natural Christians: How We Should Love Nature* (Minneapolis: Fortress Press, 1997); Ivone Gebara, *Longing for Running Water: Ecofeminism and Liberation*, trans. David Molineaux (Minneapolis: Fortress Press, 1999); Rosemary Radford Ruether, *Sexism and God-Talk: Toward a Feminist Theology, with a New Introduction*, 10th Anniversary Ed. (Boston: Beacon, 1993); Catherine Keller, *From a Broken Web: Separation, Sexism, and Self* (Boston: Beacon, 1986); Rita Nakashima

Brock, *Journeys by Heart: A Christology of Erotic Power* (New York: Crossroad, 1988); Karen Baker-Fletcher, *Sisters of Dust, Sisters of Spirit: Womanist Wordings on God and Creation* (Minneapolis: Fortress Press, 1998).

33. Richard Falk, *Religion and Humane Global Governance* (New York: Palgrave, 2001). Articulating the resistance to "globalization from above" pursued by trans-national corporations, the World Bank, and other neoliberal free trade instruments backed by the U.S. military, Falk's "globalization from below" is akin to what many are calling "democratic cosmopolitanism." It is comprised of social justice movements, alternative transnational formations, NGOs, the religious left, and environmental groups.

34 I have tried to elaborate certain spiritual and scriptural relations among uncertainty, courage, chaos, and creation in *Face of the Deep: A Theology of Becoming* (London: Routledge, 2003).

3. Territory, Terror, and Torture: Dreamreading the Apocalypse

1. Haruki Murakami, *Hard-Boiled Wonderland and the End of the World*, trans. Alfred Birnbaum (New York: Vintage, 1993 [1991]).

2. My *Apocalypse Now and Then* (Boston: Beacon, 1996) offers an in-depth analysis of the "apocalypse habit" as the western *Wirkungsgeschichte* (history of effects, Hans-Georg Gadamer's term) of the Book of Revelation. See also chapter 5 in this volume.

3. David Barsamian, Interview with Edward Said, *The Progressive*, November 2001, 41–44.

4. Richard Falk, "Ends and Means: Defining a Just War," *The Nation*, October 29, 2001, 11–15. He prefers the nomenclature "visionary terrorism" in *The Great Terror War* (New York: Olive Branch, 2003).

5. Mark Juergensmeyer, *Terror in the Mind of God: The Global Rise of Religious Violence* (Berkeley: University of California Press, 2001), 217.

6. "Remarks by the President at 2002 Graduation Exercise of the United States Military Academy, West Point, New York," Office of the Press Secretary, June 1, 2002.

7. In January 2003, essays naming and to different degrees questioning the new American empire appeared on the covers of *U.S. News & World Report*, *The New York Times Magazine*, and *Mother Jones*.

8. Reported by an admiring Bob Woodward in his book *Bush at War*, cited in "Bush's Messiah Complex," *The Progressive*, February 2003; available at: http://www.progressive.org/feb03/comm0203.html.

9. Eric Alterman, "The Roamin' Empire," *The Nation*, January 27, 2003, 10.

10. "Remarks by the President at 2002 Graduation Exercise of the United States Military Academy, West Point, New York," Office of the Press Secretary, June 1, 2002. "He may have discarded the word 'crusade,' but it's a crusade that he's on. As former Bush speechwriter [David] Frum puts it, 'War has made him a

crusader after all'" ("Bush's Messiah Complex"). This article has squarely named the phenomenon of Bush's "messianic militarism."

11. Ernst Bloch, *The Principle of Hope*, 3 vols., trans. Neville Plaice, Stephen Plaice, and Paul Knight, Studies in Contemporary German Thought (Cambridge: MIT Press, 1986).

12. "Apocalypticism was the distinctive cultural form taken by imagination in late Second Temple Jewish Society." Richard A. Horsley, *Jesus and the Spiral of Violence: Popular Jewish Resistance in Roman Palestine* (San Francisco: Harper & Row, 1987), 143.

13. "Revelation is emblematic of the difficulty of using the emperor's tools to dismantle the emperor's palace. The seer storms out of the main gates of the imperial palace, wrecking tools in hand, only to be surreptitiously swept back in through the rear entrance, having been deftly relieved of his tools at the threshold. . . . More than any other early Christian text, Revelation is replete with the language of war, conquest and empire—so much so, indeed, as to beggar description. Note in particular, however, that the promised reward for faithful Christian discipleship in Revelation is joint rulership of the Empire of empires soon destined to succeed Rome (3:21, 5:10, 20:4-6, 22:5), a messianic Empire established by means of mass-slaughter on a surreal scale (6:4.8, 8:11, 9:15.18, 11:13. 14:20, 19:15.17-21, 20:7-9) calculated to make the combined military campaigns of Julius Caesar, Augustus and all of their successors pale to insignificance by comparison." Stephen D. Moore, "Revelation," in *The Postcolonial Bible Commentary,* in Fernando F. Segovia and R. S. Sugirtharajah, eds., *A Postcolonial Community in the New Testament,* The Bible and Postcolonialism (New York: T&T Clark, forthcoming).

14. August C. Krey, *The First Crusade: The Accounts of Eye-Witnesses and Participants* (Princeton: Princeton University Press, 1921), 261–62.

15. As a New Yorker who for two months could literally smell 9/11 from my apartment, I was haunted by the hard angel's text: "Hallelujah! The smoke goes up from her forever and ever" (19:3). See chapter 1 herein.

16. Jacques Derrida, "Faith and Knowledge," in *Acts of Religion* (New York: Routledge, 2002), 67. "Religion circulates in the world, one might say, like an English word [*comme un mot anglais*] that has been to Rome and taken a detour to the United States. Well beyond its strictly capitalist or politico-military figures, a hyper-imperialist appropriation has been underway now for centuries. It imposes itself in a particularly palpable manner within the conceptual apparatus of international law and of global political rhetoric. Wherever this apparatus dominates, it articulates itself through a discourse on religion."

17. Anywhere-and-nowhere is a place postmodern civilization—its economies and its energies, its terrorism and its empire—now inhabits. The traditional territories of modern nation-states and their clear boundaries encode fading narratives, dissolving into the "shifting boundaries" of the "new planetary frontier-land." Zygmunt Bauman, "The End of Space," *Tikkun* 17, no. 2 (March/April 2002): 33–36.

18. The relation between "territory" and "terror" deserves separate consideration. Indeed territory seems derived from *terra*, or "earth," but the *Oxford English Dictionary* notes, "Etymology unsettled. . . . the original form has suggested derivation from *terrere* to frighten, whence *territor*, frightener, *territorium*, a place from which people are warned off."

19. Indeed terror may seem to be the only means of defending one's *terra* against permeation by the global, deterritorializing, and yet Americanizing consumer pop culture. But the defense is itself paradoxical, taking ever more sophisticated global form. Derrida writes of a techno-tele-iconicity that pervades, indeed makes, public space. But he reads it by means of the Abrahamisms. Derrida's "Faith and Knowledge" tracks the alliance of religion with "tele-technoscience," or globalization itself. "On the other hand it [declares] war against this power that dislodges religion" from "all its proper places, in truth from place itself, from the taking place of its truth." Hence he diagnoses an "autoimmune reaction within religion": "The auto-immunitary haunts the community . . . like the hyperbole of its own possibility" (82). Indeed this global techno-tele-iconicity is effectively deployed among the apocalyptic hyperboles of Abrahamism (the so-called fundamentalisms)—their visions fill the airwaves.

20. Edward J. Ingebretsen, S.J., *Maps of Heaven, Maps of Hell: Religious Terror as Memory from the Puritans to Stephen King* (Armonk, N.Y.: Sharpe, 1996), 200. Italics mine.

21. Falk, *Great Terror War*, cf Ch 2 note 11.

22. Ada María Isasi-Díaz, "In a Time Such as This," in *Strike Terror No More*, 299.

23. Lee Quinby, "The Gothic Fearscape of Homeland (In)Security," 2, paper presented at the Third Colloquium of Transdisciplinary Studies, "An American Empire? Globalization, War, and Religion," Drew University, September 2003; available at: http://users.drew.edu/mnausner/ttc3pdf.html. "I see this current configuration of security as the precarious marriage of Thomas Hobbes to Ann Radcliffe, or *Leviathan* as gothic enterprise. The English tradition of literary gothic, which emerged at the end of the eighteenth century, trades on experiences of terror. Filled with foreboding, with evil lurking around every corner, its benchmarks are secrecy, discoveries, and revelations that breed danger and possible salvation."

24. "In contrast to imperialism, Empire establishes no territorial center of power and does not rely on fixed boundaries or barriers. It is a decentered and deterritorializing apparatus of rule that progressively incorporates the entire global realm within its open, expanding frontiers. Empire manages hybrid identities, flexible hierarchies, and plural exchanges through modulating networks of command." Against those who in praise or condemnation locate the United States as the sole superpower, they argue that "the United States does not, and indeed no nation-state can today, form the center of an imperialist project." This is an important but distinctly pre-9/11 viewpoint, helpfully complemented by

Falk's sense of paradox. Michael Hardt and Antonio Negri, *Empire* (Cambridge: Harvard University Press, 2000), xii–xiv.

25. Elaine Scarry, *The Body in Pain: The Making and Unmaking of the World* (New York: Oxford University Press, 1985), 27.

26. Ibid., 29.

27. Ibid. 61.

28. See *The National Security Strategy of the United States of America*, September 17, 2002, 29; available at: http://www.whitehouse.gov/nsc/nss.html. This trajectory supports Noam Chomsky's designation of the United States as "a leading terrorist state" in his book *9/11* (New York: Seven Stories, 2002), 43.

29. Eyal Press, "In Torture We Trust?" *The Nation*, March 31, 2003.

30. "The photos did something else to me, as a feminist: They broke my heart. I had no illusions about the U.S. mission in Iraq—whatever exactly it is—but it turns out that I did have some illusions about women. Of the seven U.S. soldiers now charged with sickening forms of abuse in Abu Ghraib, three are women. . . . It was Harman we saw smiling an impish little smile and giving the thumbs-up sign from behind a pile of hooded, naked Iraqi men—as if to say, 'Hi Mom, here I am in Abu Ghraib!' It was England we saw with a naked Iraqi man on a leash. . . . Here, in these photos from Abu Ghraib, you have everything that the Islamic fundamentalists believe characterizes Western culture, all nicely arranged in one hideous image—imperial arrogance, sexual depravity . . . and gender equality." Barbara Ehrenreich, "What Abu Ghraib Taught Me," AlterNet (alternet.org), May 20, 2004.

31. "We have our best chance since the rise of the nation-state in the 17th century to build a world where the great powers compete in peace instead of prepare for war." *National Security Strategy*, 25:21.

32. Would the desirable alternative comprise a return to a "simple location," to sound modern boundaries, good old territorialisms, individualistic doctrines of privacy or self-possession? I do not mean to point in that direction. For in the passion of religious violence, by which the boundaries separating inside from outside, we from they, are violated, we may perhaps discern an unrecognized desire—a desire for the other, a desire that, if only recognized, might open boundaries in eros rather than assault. Late capitalism, with its Babylon of seductions, manipulates that very desire.

33. Andrew J. Bacevich, *American Empire: The Realities and Consequences of U.S. Diplomacy* (Cambridge: Harvard University Press), 2002. Bacevich opens with a revealing citation from Woodrow Wilson, October 1900: "We did not of deliberate choice undertake these new tasks which shall transform us. . . . All the world knows the surprising circumstances which thrust them upon us . . . as if part of a great preconceived plan. . . . The East is to be opened and transformed whether we will or no: the standards of the West are to be imposed upon it; nations and peoples which have stood still the centuries through . . . [will be] made part of the universal world of commerce and of ideas. . . . It is our peculiar duty . . .

to moderate the process in the interests of liberty." Bacevich defines America's "clearly defined purpose" as follows: "to preserve, and where both feasible and conducive to US interests, to expand an American imperium. Central to this strategy is a commitment to global openness—removing barriers that inhibit the movement of goods, capital, ideas, and people. Its ultimate objective is the creation of an open and integrated international order based on the principles of democratic capitalism, with the United States as the ultimate guarantor of order and enforcer of norms. . . . From the perspective of its architects, this 'strategy of openness' is benign in its intent and enlightened in its impact. On this point, the views of those subjected to the Pax Americana vary" (3).

34. Scarry, *The Body in Pain*, 53.

35. On the gender symbolism of the apocalyptic tradition, see especially chapter 4; see also *Apocalypse Now and Then*, chapter 6.

36. Richard Goldstein, "Neo-Macho Man: Pop Culture and Post-9/11 Politics," *The Nation*, March 25, 2003, 17.

37. Personal correspondence, October 5, 2003.

38. See my *Face of the Deep: A Theology of Becoming* (London: Routledge, 2003); see also chapter 8 in this volume.

39. *Just love*: Not only does this term suggest a justice tempered by mercy and warmed by compassion, but while "all you need is love," as the Beatles crooned, it is also true that love without justice is not love but abuse.

4. Ms.Calculating the Endtimes: Gender Styles of Apocalypse

1. Jeff MacGregor, "The New Pop Hero: A Mirage of Muscle and Mean," *The New York Times*, March 28, 1999, Arts and Leisure, 1ff. MacGregor's account of this ludicrously masculinizing version of the end of the world should be read in tandem with Stephen Moore's recent *God's Gym: Divine Male Bodies of the Bible* (New York: Routledge, 1998), a lucid exposé of the voracity and bulk of the apocalyptic God Himself.

2. I developed the concept of "anti-apocalypse" before encountering Lee Quinby's delightful *Antiapocalypse: Exercises in Genealogical Criticism* (Minneapolis: University of Minnesota Press, 1994), which I was able to write into my book rather late, but as a pointed illustration of the persuasive force of this position. She has followed it up with *Millennial Seduction: A Skeptic Confronts Apocalyptic Culture* (Ithaca, N.Y.: Cornell University Press, 1999). Here she performs insightful genealogies of "apocalyptic gender panic" of the Promise Keepers and of "programmed perfection" through bioengineering. Tina Pippin's *Death and Desire: The Rhetoric of Gender in the Apocalypse of John* (Louisville: Westminster John Knox, 1992) provides the collegial analogue of a feminist deconstruction of Revelation within New Testament studies proper.

3. Mary Daly, *Beyond God the Father: Toward a Philosophy of Women's Liberation* (Boston: Beacon, 1973), 96–97. Daly amplifies her vision of the apocalypse as it

transcends (absolutely) Christianity itself in *Gyn/Ecology: The Metaethics of Radical Feminism* (Boston: Beacon, 1978).

4. Cited in Leslie Wahl Rabine, "Essentialism and Its Context: Saint-Simonian and Poststructuralist Feminists," in Naomi Schor and Elizabeth Weed, eds., *The Essential Difference*, Books from Differences (Bloomington: Indiana University Press, 1994), 135.

5. "All that is a preparation for the public work of woman, but it is not a work of woman," opined Enfantin of the work of the *Tribune*. "It is we who give birth in pain to woman." See also Catherine Keller, *Apocalypse Now and Then: A Feminist Guide to the End of the World* (Boston: Beacon, 1996), 228.

6. Poem concluding Benjamin Young's *Testimony of Christ's Second Appearing* (1816), cited in Linda Mercadante, *Gender Doctrine and God: The Shakers and Contemporary Theology* (Nashville: Abingdon, 1990), 13.

7. Beryl Satter, *Each Mind a Kingdom: American Women, Sexual Purity, and the New Thought Movement, 1875–1920* (Berkeley: University of California Press, 1999), 112.

8. Ibid.

9. Ibid., 137, 195, 200.

10. In Allan A. Boesak's brilliant commentary, *Comfort and Protest: Reflections on the Apocalypse of John of Patmos* (Philadelphia: Westminster, 1987), much of which was written from a South African prison cell, he describes not a vengeful or violent but certainly a radical and militant vision of resistance to the apartheid systems, as client of the current superpower and its Babylonian system of power and commerce.

11. Nestor Miguez, "Apocalyptic and the Economy: A Reading of Revelation 18 from the Experience of Economic Exclusion," in *Reading from This Place*, vol. 2: *Social Location and Biblical Interpretation in Global Perspective*, eds. Francis F. Segovia and Mary Ann Tolbert (Minneapolis: Fortress Press, 1995), 250–62. Miguez argues "that the mythopoetic language of apocalyptic and revelatory polysemy of Scripture make it possible to read this text from the perspective of the victims of the neoliberal capitalist marketplace and its imposed instrumental logic." This is no naive identity politics, no simplistic liberation polemic.

12. Its constant presentation of Gross National Product (GNP) orthodoxy/ free-market reform as the only way, "its conviction that another alternative is bound to fail[,] also form part of this logic of death. In the end, such logic also includes self-destruction" (262). Miguez straightforwardly names his hermeneutic apocalyptic: "Apocalyptic literature stands out as the place par excellence for the expression of such a perspective" (253).

13. Elisabeth Schüssler Fiorenza, *The Book of Revelation: Justice and Judgment*, 2nd ed. (Minneapolis: Fortress Press, 1998).

14. Keller, *Apocalypse Now and Then*, 159; Catherine Keller, "The Breast, the Apocalypse, and the Colonial Journey," in *The Year 2000*, eds. Charles B. Strozier and Michael Flynn (New York: New York University Press, 1997), 42–58.

15. Letter to Torres, *Journals*. Cited in Keller, *Apocalypse Now and Then*, 159.

16. Susan Smith Nash, *Channel-Surfing the Apocalypse: A Day in the Life of the Fin-de-Millennium Mind* (Penngrove, Calif.: Avec, 1996), 29.

17. I refer the interested reader to the parables between the chapters of *Apocalypse Now and Then*.

18. Luce Irigaray, *Sexes and Genealogies*, trans. Gillian C. Gill (New York: Columbia University Press, 1993), 53.

19. See Schor and Weed, eds., *The Essential Difference*. See also Carolyn Burke, Naomi Schor, and Margaret Whitford, eds., *Engaging with Irigaray: Feminist Philosophy and Modern European Thought*, Gender and Culture (New York: Columbia University Press, 1994).

20. A wisdom text, usually considered Gnostic Christian, from the first three centuries B.C.E., "Thunder: Perfect Mind," 6:2, in *The Nag Hammadi Library*, ed. James Robinson (San Francisco: Harper & Row, 1977), 271.

5. Eyes All Over: Liberation and Deconstruction

1. Tina Pippin, *Apocalyptic Bodies: The Biblical End of the World in Text and Image* (London: Routledge, 1999), 91.

2. Catherine Keller, *Apocalypse Now and Then: A Feminist Guide to the End of the World* (Boston: Beacon, 96), 35.

3. Stephen D. O'Leary, *Arguing the Apocalypse: A Theory of Millennial Rhetoric* (New York: Oxford University Press, 1994), offers a sophisticated analysis of the function of apocalyptic language within multiple contexts of doomsday politics.

4. Jacques Derrida, *Of Grammatology*, trans. Gayatri Chakravorti Spivak (Baltimore: Johns Hopkins University Press, 1976), 158.

5. Ibid., 62.

6. Jacques Derrida, *The Post Card: From Socrates to Freud and Beyond*, trans. Alan Bass (Chicago: University of Chicago Press, 1987), 29. See also Stephen Moore's brilliant redirecting of the "postal principle" to the Gospel of Mark, in *Mark and Luke in Poststructuralist Perspectives: Jesus Begins to Write* (New Haven: Yale University Press, 1992), 38ff.

7. Derrida, *Of Grammatology*, 41.

8. "'Let's say it one more time'—deconstruction is affirmative, not a destruction or demolition," cited in John Caputo, *Deconstruction in a Nutshell: A Conversation with Jacques Derrida* (New York: Fordham, 1997), 98.

9. Nonetheless, Derrida aims his critique not at the biblical corpus but at the entire tradition of "ontotheology," which emerges in force from the confluence of Greek metaphysics with scriptural authority. *Of Grammatology*, 6ff.

10. Friedrich Nietzsche, *Genealogy* 1.15, in *The Birth of Tragedy and the Genealogy of Morals*, trans. Francis Golffing (New York: Doubleday Anchor, 1956 [1887]), 184–85.

11. On the origins of eschatology in the Zoroastrian combat myth, see Nor-

man Cohn, *Cosmos, Chaos and the World to Come: The Ancient Roots of Apocalyptic*
Faith (New Haven: Yale University Press, 1993).

12. Granted that Derrida wishes precisely to identify the two contrasts. His assimilation of writing to the freedom of the text, over and against his identification of Book with the oral authority of its "transcendental Signified," is pivotal to his critique of logocentrism. However, the resulting illusion of a convergence of Book with orality seems to me to emanate from one of his shakier arguments; cf. *Of Grammatology*, Pt. I Mark C. Taylor's dissemination of the a/theological version of Derrida's distinction of Book and Text highlights the contrast of the closure of apocalyptic writ with an open *scriptura*, writing. *Erring* (Albany: Suny University Press, 1990). But it begs the question of the apocalyptic privilege of writing itself.

13. Johann Michl, *Die Engelvorstellungen in der Apokalypse Des Hl. Johannes* (Munich: Max Hüber Verlag, 1937), 70; my translation. Michl's view typically avoids attributing divine omniscience to the creatures, while granting them more than human "*Sehvermoegen*" ("light" or "vision").

14. Catherine Gunsalus González and Justo L. González, *Revelation*, Westminster Bible Companion (Louisville: Westminster John Knox, 1997), 40.

15. See Anne Primavesi, *From Apocalypse to Genesis: Ecology, Feminism, and Christianity* (Minneapolis: Fortress Press, 1991), and Catherine Keller, "The Heat Is On: Apocalyptic Rhetoric and Climate Change," *Ecotheology* (July 1999): 40–58.

16. See the helpful discussions of *FutureNatural: Nature, Science, Culture*, ed. George Robertson, Melinda Mash, et al. (London: Routledge, 1996), especially Kate Soper, "Nature/'nature,'" 22–34.

17. Derrida, *Of Grammatology*, 42.

18. "*Différence*," in *A Derrida Reader: Between the Blinds*, ed. Peggy Kamuf (New York: Columbia University Press), 75.

19. See the unique and accessible exegesis of ecologist Bill McKibben, *The Comforting Whirlwind: God, Job and the Scale of Creation* (Grand Rapids: Eerdmans, 1994).

20. J. William Whedbee, *The Bible and the Comic Vision* (Minneapolis: Fortress Press, 2002), 221–62.

21. D. H. Lawrence, *Apocalypse* (New York: Viking, 1980), 51; see also Keller, *Apocalypse Now and Then*, 50.

22. Stephen Moore, *God's Gym: Divine Male Bodies of the Bible* (New York: Routledge, 1996), 3.

23. Ibid., 27.

24. Donna J. Haraway, *Modest_Witness@Second_Millennium.FemaleMan_Meets_OncoMouse: Feminism and Technoscience* (New York: Routledge, 1997), 45.

25. Elisabeth Schüssler Fiorenza, *The Book of Revelation: Justice and Judgment*, 2nd ed. (Minneapolis: Fortress Press, 1998); see also Keller, *Apocalypse Now and Then*, 31.

26. Daniel Boyarin, *Intertextuality and the Reading of Midrash* (Bloomington: Indiana University Press, 1990), 12, 94.

27. The Bible and Culture Collective, *The Postmodern Bible* (New Haven: Yale University Press, 1995), 130.

28. Boyarin, *Intertextuality*, 94.

29. See Rachel Elior, "The Concept of God in Hekhalot Literature," in Joseph Dan, ed., *Studies in Jewish Thought*, Binah vol. 2 (New York: Praeger, 1989), 97–120.

30. Boyarin, *Intertextuality*.

31. Schüssler Fiorenza, *The Book of Revelation*.

32. Homi K. Bhabha's term; see chapter 3 in this volume.

33. Pippin, *Apocalyptic Bodies*, 125; see also *Death and Desire: The Rhetoric of Gender in the Apocalypse of John* (Louisville: Westminster John Knox, 1992).

34. Moore, *God's Gym*, 12.

35. Ibid., 125.

36. Cited in Keller, *Apocalypse Now and Then*, 246.

37. Ibid., 247.

38. Despite even a great feminist New Testament scholar's (Elisabeth Schüssler Fiorenza) love of this text as the primary New Testament text of justice.

39. See Keller, *Apocalypse Now and Then*, which documents this theme extensively in the chapter on gender.

40. The Bible and Culture Collective, *The Postmodern Bible*, 141.

41. I am honored to be criticized by Pippin as "submitting to the authority of the biblical text" (*Apocalyptic Bodies*, 8) and by Ted Peters as scorning that same authority (Review of *Apocalypse Now and Then* in *Theology Today* 54 [July 1997]: 243–46), both of whom I appreciate for their ability to criticize without dismissal—itself a counter-apocalyptic skill.

42. Jacques Derrida, "Of an Apocalyptic Tone Newly Adapted in Philosophy," in *Derrida and Negative Theology*, trans. John P. Leavy, ed. Harold Coward and Toby Foshay (Albany: State University of New York Press, 1992), 58.

43. Ibid., 66.

44. Ibid., 54.

45. Friedrich Nietzsche, *The Antichrist*, trans. Anthony M. Ludovici (Amherst, N.Y.: Prometheus, 2000).

46. Derrida, "Of an Apocalyptic Tone," 59.

47. Ibid.

48. Ibid.

49. Ibid., 67.

50. Bible and Culture Collective, *The Postmodern Bible*, 138.

51. John D. Caputo, *The Prayers and Tears of Jacques Derrida: Religion without Religion* (Bloomington: Indiana University Press, 1997), 95.

52. Ibid., 98.

53. Ibid., 100.

54. Luce Irigaray, *An Ethics of Sexual Difference*, trans. Carolyn Burke and Gillian C. Gill (Ithaca, N.Y.: Cornell University Press, 1991 [1984]), 148.

55. Ibid.

56. Ibid., 149.

especially and most powerfully the concluding christological construction of *The Marine Lover of Friedrich Nietzsche*, trans. Gillian C. Gill (New York: Columbia University Press, 1991); also *Sexes and Genealogies*, trans. Gillian C. Gill (New York: Columbia University Press, 1993); and most readably *I Love to You: Sketch for a Felicity within History*, trans. Alison Martin (New York: Routledge, 1996).

58. Luce Irigaray, *The Forgetting of Air in Martin Heidegger*, trans. Mary Beth Mader (Austin: University of Texas Press, 1999), 178.

59. Derrida, "Of an Apocalyptic Tone," 52.

60. The translation is from Martin S. Cohen's "The Song of Songs and the Shicur Qomah" (p. 9), an unpublished paper that Stephen Moore has generously passed on to me.

61. "The ascription of form and beauty to God are apparently daring; nonetheless, a careful analysis of the concept of beauty in hekhalot literature reveals that the descriptions are based on cosmic beauty, on the majesty of the universe, and on the power of universal natural forces" ("The Concept of God," in *Studies in Jewish Thought*, 107). The attempt to perceive and measure a body of God in this early Jewish mysticism does seem to anticipate the beauty and dimensionality discernible through the Hubble telescope and other quite nonmystical tools of the current golden age in astronomy. "God put his hand on me and blessed me. . . . I was raised the height and breadth of the world and given 72 wings . . . each wing the size of the world, and on each wing there were 365 eyes, each eye the size of the sun. No luminescence or brightness was omitted" (ibid., 107–8).

62. Michl, *Die Engelvorstellungen in der Apokalypse*, 71.

6. Everywhere and Nowhere: Postcolonial Positions

1. Patricia J. Williams, "In-Laws and Outlaws," *Arizona Law Review* 46/199 (2004): 199–209.

2. Zygmunt Bauman, "The End of Space," *Tikkun*, 17, no. 2 (March/April 2002), 33ff.

3. Laura E. Donaldson and Kwok Pui-Lan, *Postcolonialism, Feminism, and Religious Discourse* (London: Routledge, 2002), and Marcella Althaus Reid, *Indecent Theologies: Theological Perversions in Sex, Gender, and Politics* (London: Routledge, 2001). As this goes to press, Kwok Pui-Lan's *Postcolonial Imagination and Feminist Theology* (Louisville: Westminster John Knox, 2004) has been released. Theologians at Drew University attempted to fill the gap by collecting the essays of *Postcolonial Theologies: Divinity and Empire*, Catherine Keller, Michael Nausner, and Mayra Rivera (St. Louis: Chalice, 2004).

4. Michael Hardt and Antonio Negri may criticize postcolonial theory as a mere symptom of passage to empire, able to diagnose and transgress the modern spatiality of tightly bounded nation-states but not the postmodern empire, which in its globalizing fluidity of capital and resources has already itself subverted

the modern state polity. See their book *Empire* (Cambridge: Harvard University Press, 2000).

5. Robert J. C. Young, *Postcolonialism: An Historical Introduction* (Oxford: Blackwell, 2001).

6. Gayatri Chakravorty Spivak, *A Critique of Postcolonial Reason: Toward a History of the Vanishing Present* (Cambridge: Harvard University Press, 1999).

7. See also more recent contributions by Roland Boer, *Last Stop before Antarctica: The Bible and Postcolonialism in Australia* (Sheffield: Sheffield University Press, 2001); Tat-Siong Benny Liew, *Politics of Parousia: Reading Mark Inter(con)textually*, Biblical Interpretation (Leiden and Boston: Brill, 1999); Fernando F. Segovia, "Biblical Critics and Postcolonial Studies: Toward a Postcolonial Optic," in *The Postcolonial Bible*, edited by P. S. Sugirtharajah (Sheffield: Sheffield University Press, 1998); Stephen D. Moore, "Mark and Empire: 'Zealot' and Postcolonial Readings," in *Postcolonial Theologies*, Keller et al.; and Musa W. Dube, *Postcolonial Feminist Interpretation of the Bible* (St. Louis: Chalice, 2000).

8. Ivone Gebara, *Longing for Running Water: Ecofeminism and Liberation*, trans. David Molineaux (Minneapolis: Fortress Press, 1999), 46.

9. Homi K. Bhabha, *The Location of Culture* (London: Routledge, 1994).

10. Chela Sandoval, *Methodology of the Oppressed*, Theory Out of Bounds, vol. 18 (Minneapolis: University of Minnesota Press, 2000), 183.

11. Rey Chow, *The Protestant Ethnic and the Spirit of Capitalism* (New York: Columbia University Press, 2002), 47.

12. See also chapter 11 in Néstor Míguez, "The Old Creation in the New, the New Creation in the Old," in *Wesleyan Perspectives on the New Creation*, ed. M. Douglas Meeks (Nashville: Abingdon, 2004), 53–72.

13. Richard A. Falk, *The Great Terror War* (New York: Olive Branch, 2003), xiv.

14. Zoé Oldenbourg, *The Crusades*, trans. Anne Carter (London: Weidenfeld & Nicolson, 1966), 208, cited in Karen Armstrong, *Holy War: The Crusades and Their Impact on Today's World* (New York: Anchor, 1988), 187.

15. See Virginia Burrus, *The Making of a Heretic: Gender, Authority, and the Priscillianist Controversy*, Transformation of the Classical Heritage (Berkeley: University of California Press, 1995).

16. Chow, *The Protestant Ethnic*, 185–86.

17. Sandoval, *Methodology*, 181; see also 2, 4.

7. The Love Supplement: Christianity and Empire

1. Michael Hardt and Antonio Negri, *Empire* (Cambridge: Harvard University Press, 2000), 202.

2. "Anglobalization" is a nifty neologism for the history of globalization as promoted by Great Britain and its colonies. Niall Ferguson, *Empire: The Rise and Demise of the British World Order and the Lessons of Global Power* (New York: Basic Books, 2002), xxvi.

3. Zygmunt Bauman, "Living and Dying in the Planetary Frontier-Land," *Tikkun* (March/April 2002).

4. Donald H. Rumsfeld, the U.S. Secretary of Defense, warned that this war "will not be waged by a grand alliance united to defeat an axis of hostile powers. Instead, it will involve floating coalitions of countries, which may change and evolve." (*International Herald Tribune*, September 28, 2001).

5. Bauman, "Living and Dying," 42.

6. See Michael Nausner's meditation on the theological space of the boundary in *Postcolonial Theologies: Divinity and Empire*, ed. Catherine Keller, Michael Nausner, and Mayra Rivera (St. Louis: Chalice, 2004).

7. Bauman, "Living and Dying," 42.

8. For Jacques Derrida's reflections on ethics as hospitality, see especially Jacques Derrida, *On Cosmopolitanism and Forgiveness: Thinking in Action* (London: Routledge, 2001), 16f.

9. Hardt and Negri, *Empire*, xii.

10. Ibid., xii, xiii.

11. Ibid., 203. Recent corporate revelations give credence to their construal of corruption as not an aberration but the "very essence and modus operandi" of empire. And the post-9/11 military aggression of the United States—which as a national sovereignty is not quite identical with this new Empire—confirms their expectation of a new form of power without boundaries, whose military might demands at first a transnational moral coding ("just war," UN sanction, etc.), only that its might may come to determine the new codes of global right.

12. Hardt and Negri, *Empire*, xii.

13. Ibid., 138.

14. Ibid., 203.

15. Ibid., 146.

16. Ibid., 138.

17. "Resistance," writes Bhabha, "is not necessarily an oppositional act of political intention, nor is it the simple negation or exclusion of the 'content' of another culture, as a difference once perceived. It is the effect of an ambivalence produced within the rules of recognition of dominating discourses." Homi K. Bhabha, *The Location of Culture* (London: Routledge, 1994), 110.

18. Hardt and Negri, *Empire*, 145.

19. Words like *imperialism* and *neocolonialism* have over decades signified the colonizing dynamics that operate within the "postcolonial" era, that is, the era that follows the political independence of the European colonies. "Globalization" names the more recent effect of transnational corporations in the constitution of a new economic order. But the 9/11 events may have revealed (apocalypse intended) the singular political-military role of the United States in relation to the global economy of which it has been the major but not the solo player. For a lucid elaboration of the historical relations of "postcolonialism" to anti-colonial movements as well as to ongoing processes of colonization and imperialism, see Robert J. C. Young, *Postcolonialism: An Historical Introduction* (Oxford: Blackwell, 2001).

20. "Money circulates with little restraint, and world powers demand 'open markets' for their manufactured goods, especially in relation to subordinate countries (though they largely protect and subsidize their own production). In contrast, the policies of migration are severely restricted, so that people are prevented from following their money. It is interesting to note that while the capitalist world rejoiced over the falling of the Berlin Wall and claimed it as a triumph of liberty and democracy, it has continued building other walls, not only symbolic but also physical walls have been built along the borders of rich and poor countries—the Mexican-USA border, for example—around the protected neighborhoods of the rich within famished countries, and around the 'outlawed' Palestinian territories, rendering them no better than concentration camps. Since the market cannot integrate the poor, they are excluded outside the walls." Néstor Míguez, "The Old Creation in the New, the New Creation in the Old," in *Wesleyan Perspectives on the New Creation*, ed. M. Douglas Meeks (Nashville: Abingdon, 2004), 57.

21. Hardt and Negri, *Empire*, 192–93.

22. Ibid., 218.

23. Ibid., 146.

24. Bhabha, *Location of Culture*, 7.

25. Ibid., 218.

26. John Milbank, *The Word Made Strange: Theology, Language, Culture* (Oxford: Blackwell, 1997), 285.

27. John Milbank, "Sovereignty, Empire, Capital, and Terror," in *Strike Terror No More: Theology, Ethics, and the New War*, ed. Jon L. Berquist (St. Louis: Chalice, 2002).

28. Ibid., 66.

29. Ibid., 67.

30. Ibid.

31. Young, *Postcolonialism*, 32.

32. Assisted by the historicist and comparativist work of Henry Maine. Milbank, "Sovereignty," 67.

33. Ibid., 74.

34. Ibid., 75; italics added.

35. I find the proposal inviting at one level—I too feel a spiritual affinity to the neoplatonically tinged mysticism of the Kabbalists and the Sufis. But Milbank's theology always swerves sharply from the bottomless depths of these mysticisms to their foundational reason. Here Milbank's disdain for the poststructuralist discovery of negative theology chokes off a more complex examination of these shared mysticisms, in their own subversive capacities.

36. Postcolonial theory is dependent upon that deconstructive discourse; indeed it reads poststructuralism as an internal deconstruction of the Eurocentric itself. Robert Young locates deconstruction, especially the Algerian Jew Derrida, within the context of the Algerian war of independence, in its tremendous influ-

ence on generations of French intellectuals. "What is deconstruction a deconstruction of?" asks Young. "The answer would be, of the concept, the authority,
and assumed primacy of, the category of 'the West.' Postmodernism can best be
defined as European culture's awareness that it is no longer the unquestioned
and dominant center of the world." Robert J. C. Young, *White Mythologies: Writing
History and the West*, 2nd ed. (London: Routledge, 2004), 19.

37. Bhabha, *Location of Culture*, 89.

38. Richard Falk, "Will the Empire Be Fascist?" in his *The Declining World Order:
America's Imperial Geopolitics*, Global Horizons (New York: Routledge, 2004).

39. Milbank, *Word Made Strange*, 269.

40. Ibid., 270.

41. But he excoriates the unorthodox immanentism of the ecological theologies. I do not dismiss his criticisms. Perhaps liberation theology has operated in
an eschatological history indifferent to the nonhuman constituents of material
space, reflecting the indifference of the class system to the effects of landlessness
upon the peasant. But no more than Hardt and Negri and most postcolonial
theory does Milbank attend to ecological space.

42. Milbank, *Word Made Strange*, 285.

43. Ibid., 50.

44. See John Milbank, *Theology and Social Theory: Beyond Secular Reason*, Sign-
posts in Theology (Cambridge, Mass.: Blackwell, 1991).

45. Eliot A. Cohen, "A Tale of Two Secretaries," *Foreign Affairs* 81, no. 3 (May
2002): 46.

46. For an excellent analysis of the effects of Straussian classicism in contemporary politics and its influence on figures such as Paul Wolfowitz, William Kristol,
and Abram Schulz, see Mark Lewis Taylor, "Liberals, Neocons and the Christian
Right: Options for Pro-Active Christian Witness in Post-9/11 USA," *Constellation:
Journal of Progressive Christian Thought*, December 2003, Center for Progressive
Christianity; available at http://www.tcpc.org/resources/constellation/fall_03/
taylor.htm. A key text is Leo Strauss, *The Rebirth of Classical Political Rationalism*,
ed. Thomas L. Pangle (Chicago: University of Chicago Press, 1989), 6.

47. Michael J. Glennon, "Why the Security Council Failed," *Foreign Affairs* 82,
no. 3 (May/June 2003): 34. In *The War over Iraq: Saddam's Tyranny and America's
Mission* (San Francisco: Encounter Books, 2003), William Kristol and Lawrence
Kaplan write: "The alternative to American leadership," they write, "is a chaotic,
Hobbesian world where there is no authority to thwart aggression, ensure peace
and security or enforce international norms."

48. Gayatri Chakravorty Spivak, *A Critique of Postcolonial Reason: Toward a History of the Vanishing Present* (Cambridge: Harvard University Press, 1999), 382.

49. See "Afterword" in ibid.

50. Derrida's sense of justice is avowedly "haunted" by the messianic, as it
echoes in the unfulfilled promise of both democracy and communism: "this
absolutely undetermined messianic hope at its heart, this eschatological relation

to the to-come of an event and of a singularity, of an alterity that cannot be anticipated. Awaiting without horizon of the wait, awaiting what one does not expect yet or any longer, hospitality without reserve." Jacques Derrida, *Specters of Marx: The State of the Debt, the Work of Mourning, and the New International* (New York: Routledge, 1994), 65.

51. Spivak, *Critique*, 380.

52. Ibid., 361.

53. Ibid., 380.

54. Gayatri Chakravorty Spivak, *Death of a Discipline*, Wellek Library Lectures in Critical Theory (New York: Columbia University Press, 2003), 72, 74. "The globe is in our computers. No one lives there. It allows us to think that we can aim to control it. The planet is a species of alterity, belonging to another system; and yet we inhabit it, on loan" (72). Thanks to Mayra Rivera for apprising me of this ever more ecotheological development.

55. Spivak, *Critique*, 386.

56. Ibid., 382.

57. Ibid.; italics added.

58. Ibid.

59. The British process theologian Norman Pittenger had in my seminary days been lecturing about nature as "super"—in the then-youthful colloquialism. Sally McFague amplifies this anti-dualistic trope. See Sallie McFague, *Super, Natural Christians: How We Should Love Nature* (Minneapolis: Fortress Press, 1997).

60. Spivak, *Critique*, 382.

61. Latin American critics have relentlessly exposed these habits; see Ivone Gebara, *Longing for Running Water: Ecofeminism and Liberation*, trans. David Molineaux (Minneapolis: Fortress Press, 1999), and Marcella Althaus-Reid, *Indecent Theology: Theological Perversions in Sex, Gender and Politics* (London: Routledge, 2000).

62. Spivak, *Critique*, 388.

63. Such hybrids have long provided the subject matter of much of the work of religious ethnography, including that advanced by Karen McCarthy Brown and Ada María Isasi-Díaz, even as the thought-forms they disclose have nonaccidental affinities to the evolution of theological panentheism.

64. Spivak, *Critique*, 383; italics added.

65. Ibid.

66. Thomas Mann, *The Magic Mountain,* a new translation from the German by John E. Woods (New York: Vintage, 1996), 590.

67. Míguez, "The Old Creation in the New, the New Creation in the Old."

68. I have distinguished between crypto-, retro-, and neo-apocalypse in the ultimate interest not of an anti- but a counter-apocalypse, in my book *Apocalypse Now and Then: A Feminist Guide to the End of the World* (Boston: Beacon, 1996).

69. I have elsewhere read "in depth" this *tehom* of Gen. 1:2. See chapter 8 of this volume and also Catherine Keller, *Face of the Deep: A Theology of Becoming* (London: Routledge, 2002).

70. Charles Hartshorne, Grace Jantzen, Sallie McFague.

71. "The term 'blowback,' which officials of the Central Intelligence Agency first invented for their own internal use, is starting to circulate among students of international relations. It refers to unintended consequences of policies that were kept secret from the American people. What the daily press reports as the malign acts of 'terrorists,' or 'drug lords,' or 'rogue states' or 'illegal arms merchants' often turn out to be blowback from earlier American operations." Chalmers A. Johnson, *Blowback: The Costs and Consequences of American Empire* (New York: Metropolitan, 2000), 8.

72. Trinh T. Minh-ha, "An Acoustic Journey," in *Rethinking Borders,* ed. John C. Welchman (Minneapolis: University of Minnesota Press, 1996), 16.

8. The Democracy of Creation: Chaosmos and Counter-Apocalypse

1. From an interview with George W. Bush by Bob Woodward, in *Plan of Attack* (New York: Simon and Schuster, 2003).

2. This argument is developed fully in my book *Face of the Deep: A Theology of Becoming* (London: Routledge, 2003), chap. 11. For an introduction to chaos theory, beyond James Gleich's *Chaos* (New York: Viking, 1987), see the delightful popularizations and applications of chaos theory by John Briggs and F. David Peat, *Turbulent Mirror: An Illustrated Guide to Chaos Theory and the Science of Wholeness* (New York: Harper & Row, 1989), and idem, *Seven Life Lessons of Chaos* (New York: HarperCollins, 1999). Highly readable scientists of chaos include biologist Stuart Kauffman, *At Home in the Universe: The Search for Laws of Self-Organization and Complexity* (New York: Oxford University Press, 1995); and physicist Per Bak, *How Nature Works: The Science of Self Organized Criticality* (New York: Springer-Verlag, 1996).

3. At most, God "calls into being the things that are not" (Rom. 4:17), which posits a strong sense of God as source of radical newness; see also Heb. 11:3; 2 Macc. 7:28; and John 1:1 for the other passages used to back up the *ex nihilo* view. Biblical texts may ignore the chaos or dread and rebuke its waters, but they never exclude the chaotic initial conditions obtaining "when God created."

4. For the expanded version of this historical itinerary, see Keller, *Face of the Deep*, Part Two. In interpreting the Gnostic and patristic exegesis of Gen. 1:1-2, I draw upon Gerhard May, *Creatio ex Nihilo: The Doctrine of "Creation out of Nothing" in Early Christian Thought*, trans. A. S. Worrall (Edinburgh: T & T Clark, 1994). Augustine's *Confessions* is the key text for his hermeneutical pluralism vis-à-vis Genesis 1. And my engagement with Barth centers largely on his *Church Dogmatics*, 3 vols. (Edinburgh: T & T Clark, 1936–1975), III:1.

5. Alexander Heidel, *The Babylonian Genesis: A Complete Translation of All the Published Cuneiform Tablets of the Various Babylonian Creation Stories* (Chicago: University of Chicago Press, 1951).

6. In an intensely readable book, *Religion and Its Monsters*, Tim Beal notes of Tiamat that "the cosmos is imagined as her filleted corpse." In relation to her death, which by the end of the poem the poet is hoping anxiously to prolong as long as possible, he quips, "It is difficult to keep a good monster down." Timothy K. Beal, *Religion and Its Monsters* (New York: Routledge, 2002), 18.

7. Luce Irigaray, *Marine Lover of Friedrich Nietzsche*, trans. Gillian C. Gill (New York: Columbia University Press, 1991), 49.

8. "Remarks by the President at 2002 Graduation Exercise of the United States Military Academy, West Point, New York," Office of the Press Secretary, June 1, 2002, italics added; see also chapter 2 of this volume.

9. Zygmunt Bauman, "Living and Dying in the Planetary Frontier-Land," *Tikkun* (March/April 2002), 35; see also chapter 7 of this volume.

10. Robert Kaplan, "Supremacy by Stealth," *Atlantic Monthly*, July/August 2003.

11. Thomas Hobbes, *The Leviathan*, cited in Beal, *Religion and Its Monsters*, 99.

12. Hobbes cited in ibid., 100.

13. Bill McKibben, *The Comforting Whirlwind: God, Job, and the Scale of Creation* (Grand Rapids: Eerdmans, 1994), 54ff.

14. Translation by Stephen Mitchell, *Job* (New York: HarperCollins, 1992).

15. Norman C. Habel, *The Book of Job: A Commentary* (Philadelphia: Westminster, 1985), 538.

16. Cited in *Job*, ed. and trans. Marvin H. Pope (Garden City: Doubleday, 1973), 293.

17. Carol Newsom, "Job," in *The Women's Bible Commentary*, ed. Carol A. Newsom and Sharon H. Ringe (Louisville: Westminster John Knox, 1992), 136.

18. Ivone Gebara, *Out of the Depths: Women's Experience of Evil and Salvation*, trans. Ann Patrick Ware (Minneapolis: Fortress Press, 2002), 172–73. See also Rosemary Radford Ruether, *Sexism and God-Talk: Toward a Feminist Theology, with a New Introduction*, 10th Anniversary Ed. (Boston: Beacon, 1993), and Sallie McFague, *The Body of God: An Ecological Theology* (Minneapolis: Fortress Press, 1993).

19. *Pentateuch with Targum, Onkelos, Haphtaroth and Rashi's Commentary: Genesis*, trans. M. Rosenbaum and A. M. Silbermann (New York: Hebrew Publishing, 1965), 2–3.

20. Briggs and Peat, *Turbulent Mirror*, 52.

21. "De Docta Ignorantia," in *Nicholas of Cusa: Selected Spiritual Writings*, trans. H. Lawrence Bond (Mahwah, N.Y.: Paulist, 1997), 125–26.

22. Henry Vaughan (1622–95), "The Night," *Oxford Book of English Verse*, (Oxford: Oxford University Press, 1999), 198–99.

23. bell hooks, "An Aesthetic of Blackness," in *Yearning: Race, Gender and Cultural Politics* (Boston: South End Press, 1990), 113.

24. Trinh T. Minh-ha, "An Acoustic Journey," in *Rethinking Borders*, ed. John C. Welchman (Minneapolis: University of Minnesota Press, 1996), 16.

25. Gebara, *Out of the Depths*, 132.

26. Ibid., 58, 172.

27. Angelus Silesius, *Cherubinischer Wandersmann* (Ein Siedeln: Johannes Verlag, 1980), 38, my translation.

Index